T0196547

HOLY POLITICS

HOLY POLITICS

A Christian's Guide
to Political Discourse

It's in the Bible;
you can look it up.

Nancy Smithson Summerlin

Print information available on the last page.

Rev. date: 12/02/2016

To order additional copies of this book, contact:
Xlibris
1-888-795-4274
www.Xlibris.com
Orders@Xlibris.com
746628

CONTENTS

For

Lewis Miller Smithson

Introduction

Growing up in a Christian home, I went to Sunday school, sang in the choir, participated in youth groups, spent summers at church camp, and attended worship twice on Sunday and once in the middle of the week. At the heart of everything was the Bible that has been a source of inspiration, wisdom, comfort, and ethical challenge through my growing years, management career, seminary studies, daily devotions, and weekly sermon preparation. That's why I want to share something important about what it means for me to be a Christian in the current political climate.

During the past few election cycles, it seems that some candidates, elected officials, and their supporters have *used* God to increase poll numbers, *misused* Scripture to support favored policies and positions, or *claimed* Christianity as a reason to mistrust people (*even other Christians!*) who may have different ideas and beliefs, or who just get in the way of unbridled political ambition. More often than not, members of the news media report these statements (*over and over in a 24-7 news cycle*) without question or comment, and ratings go up. As a citizen, I am disturbed that religion is sometimes reduced to political "spin" in ways that are both cynical and reckless. As a pastor, in the business of talking about God, I am both disappointed and alarmed by the use of incendiary language in the name of Christianity. Why? Because Scripture is very clear: *what* we say to—and about—each other, and *how* we say it, does matter.

This has nothing to do with political correctness and has everything to do with what Jesus said about how we should communicate with each other—even when it comes to politics:

> *Listen and understand: it is not what goes into the*
> *mouth that defiles a person, but it is what comes*

out of the mouth that defiles, [because] what comes out of the mouth proceeds from the heart, and this is what defiles. For out of the heart come evil intentions, murder, adultery, theft, false witness, slander. These are what defile a person. (Matthew 15:10–11, 19–20a)

In other words, when the ideas that come through our hearts and out of our mouths communicate bad intentions, encourage violence, and result in falsehood and slander, then our words dishonor us when we speak; and we dishonor all those who hear and are influenced by what we say.

Listen to how the Apostle Paul weighed in on the matter:[1]

Let no evil talk come out of your mouths, but only what is useful for building up, as there is need, so that your words may give grace to those who hear. (Ephesians 4:29)

Of course, there are few (*if any*) legal consequences for ignoring what Scripture says about words and how they are used. But when people claim to be Christians—when politicians and media personalities make that claim as part of their credentials—they *should* pay attention to what they say and do by putting biblical teaching before ego, pride, ambition, poll numbers, and TV ratings. And when citizens claim that being a Christian is part of who we are and how we filter information, then *we* have a responsibility to evaluate the messages we send and receive with thoughtful consideration of the same standards—around the coffeepot at work, across the kitchen table at home, and on social media everywhere.

---

[1]   See also Colossians 3:8.

Politicians, surrogates, reporters, and commentators have unique opportunities (*and skills*) to influence public opinion. These opportunities also come with professional responsibilities. When religion becomes part of the narrative, they have a greater responsibility *to avoid* communicating bad intentions, falsehoods, and slander; and *to call out others* who are speaking this way while campaigning and governing.

The chapters that follow will discuss how Judeo-Christian principles found in Scripture apply to current political issues. This information is not intended to replace freedom of thought or to influence voting choices. It is, however, meant to provide biblical insights for those who claim that Christianity is part of how they make decisions – either as citizens or as elected leaders. And although I am the one writing and assembling what you will read, there is a genuine attempt to keep personal biases to a minimum by focusing more on what is found in the Bible—not just a verse or two here and there, but the cover-to-cover witness you can read in passages that are included in the text and in footnote citations that you may look up for yourself.

Why Christianity?

Well, because that's where the political focus seems to be right now. And because that's who I am. As you read (*and look up*) what the Bible says about such issues as fear, anger, wealth, poverty, and immigration, you may be surprised at what you find. I was. Like many people, what I thought I knew about the Bible started with Sunday school teachers and preachers who told me what it meant. And they, often, were passing on what other people had told them. Sometimes, even the most important information can be miscommunicated this way for several reasons:

1. As human beings, we tend to hear what we *want to hear* or what we *expect to hear* based on what we *think we know* already.

2. While reading the Bible, we generally assign meanings to words that are consistent with the meanings those words have for us today, without considering what they said in the original Hebrew and Greek.

3. Selected verses that seem to be about current issues sometimes are lifted out of the historical, social, and theological context of the Bible and then are inserted into what is swirling around us today—sometimes jumbling the big picture God has given us as a timeless guide for living.

Over the years, I have come to accept that human beings often are in danger of taking *from* the Bible what we bring *to* the Bible; and that without realizing it, we can shape the Word of God to fit our unique personal and cultural experiences and preferences. For example, looking through the lenses of personal experience can cause an intelligent, well-educated news personality to say that Santa Claus should not be represented in any racial or ethnic way other than white because Santa was white. And, by the way, Jesus was white also. Of course, if Jesus was white, that also must mean God is white.

The proof given for Santa's race was the movie *Miracle on 34th Street.* I suppose the proof about Jesus would be the picture (*hanging in many churches as far back as I can remember*) that shows him with light skin, blue eyes, and flowing light-brown hair. The proof about God probably would be Michelangelo's fresco on the ceiling of the Sistine Chapel of a muscular white God with a flowing white beard reaching out to Adam.

All this ignores what history and theology tell us: St. Nicholas, who lived in the fourth century, was from modern-day Turkey and is depicted in icons with various shades of skin from light to dark. Jesus of Nazareth, while being the Son of God, was incarnate (*lived in the flesh*) as a first-century Palestinian Jew and probably would have looked like other Palestinian Jews, with dark eyes, dark curly hair, and brown skin. The Creator God is Spirit[2] and has no physical human features.

Reading Scripture only through personal experiences can be misleading.

Bit by bit, we start to believe that God is like us: thinks the same way we think, believes what we believe, likes the people we like, dislikes the people we dislike, and wants for us what we want for ourselves. In other words, we gradually begin to create God in our own image. And if we come to believe that God is *only* like us, we can start to mistrust and become suspicious of other groups who are *not* like us—even those who worship the same God but whose lives have been shaped differently by how, when, and where they grew up; who their people are; where and when they were educated; what churches they attend or attended; and how they live their lives, either by choice or necessity.

It is this tendency that I struggle against personally and speak out against publicly as a reminder that God is not like us. God is holy and divine and grace filled and just and merciful and steadfast and loving and all manner of wisdom and goodness that we can barely comprehend. God is God; and we are not God. But we—who are created in God's image, both of us male and female[3]—are called to try, as best we can, to live and communicate as the people God created us to be. We are especially called to practice the same kindness and openness Jesus modeled for us when his ministry reached out to people from different political, ethnic, and cultural backgrounds, such as the tax-collector Zacchaeus, the Samaritan woman at the well, and the Roman centurion whose servant he healed. When we learn to communicate with other people as God intended, we are more likely to reduce our own noise level and hear the message God is speaking to us in this time and place.

---

[2] John 4:24.

[3] **Genesis 1:27,** "So God created humankind in his image, in the image of God he created them; male and female he created them."

Summary: Whatever we do in our private and professional lives should follow the laws by which we all have agreed to live. And if we have any hope of coexisting with a minimum amount of chaos and violence, we may want to consider treating each other with some basic decency and old-fashioned manners. However, when we take on the name of Christian, we also have taken on a higher standard for behavior and mutual discourse—a standard that has been given to us by Jesus Christ. *What* we say to and about each other—and *how* we say it—does matter if we believe what he says:

> *I tell you, on the day of judgment you will have to give an account for every careless word you utter; for by your words you will be justified, and by your words you will be condemned.* (Matthew 12:36–37)

So where do we find that higher standard for mutual discourse? It's in the Bible. You can look it up!

Chapter 1

God and Fear (*and Anxiety*)

When we live in fear,
we are not living in faith.

Fear is a useful emotion that alerts us to danger. It is part of our primitive heritage when survival depended on knowing that a saber-tooth tiger was crouching just outside the cave. However, when this fight-or-flight response to immediate threats is encouraged and fed by constant messages that say we should be afraid of everything (*and everyone*) around us, it's hard to make the choice between fight-or-flight. It's hard to make any choice under the persistent influence of fear and anxiety. Dwelling on fear and allowing it to become the focus of our lives is more than debilitating; it simply *is not Christian.*

Sadly, many people associate God with fear.

The very name of God arouses fear in far too many people: fear of punishment, fear of not going to heaven, and fear of going to hell. A lot of sermons dwell on fear because this message has been known, over the years, to fill pews—and offering plates! However, if the only reason for going to church or trying to live good lives is the fear of not getting something we want (*or getting something we don't want!*), we miss the most important reason for doing anything—the joy of living faithfully in God's presence each day.

Many people associate God with fear because the Bible, especially the Old Testament, says we should "fear the Lord." And in English, the word *fear* means "being afraid." In Hebrew, however, the word we translate as "fear" has several different meanings. When the Bible talks about being afraid of dangerous people (*even wild animals and extreme weather events*), the meaning is "fear" or "dread." When we read "fear the Lord," the word means "reverence," "awe," "amazement," "devotion," or "worship." One good example of this fear is in the story about Jacob's dream at Bethel:

> *Then Jacob woke from his sleep and said, "Surely the LORD is in this place—and I did not know it!" And he was afraid, and said, "How awesome*

> *is this place! This is none other than the house*
> *of God, and this is the gate of heaven." So Jacob*
> *rose early in the morning, and he took the stone*
> *that he had put under his head and set it up for*
> *a pillar and poured oil on the top of it.* (Genesis
> 28:16–18)

Jacob's fear was not the same as being afraid of a wild animal or dreading an encounter with someone who might do him harm, even though both could have happened to him while he was sleeping alone in the wilderness. Instead, his fear was a sense of awe when he realized he had been in the presence of God. And his awe moved him to worship! The Bible is full of occasions that are both comforting and encouraging when people are told to embrace the "fear [*awe, reverence, amazement, devotion, worship*] of the Lord," such as:[4]

> *Let all the earth fear the LORD; let all the*
> *inhabitants of the world stand in awe of him. For*
> *he spoke, and it came to be; he commanded, and*
> *it stood firm.* (Psalm 33:8–9)

> *O taste and see that the LORD is good; happy are*
> *those who take refuge in him. O fear the LORD,*
> *you his holy ones, for those who fear him have no*
> *want.* (Psalm 34:8–9)

Even so, the human experience of raw fear is an honest emotion, even in the Bible.

Adam was afraid when he became aware of his nakedness.[5] Hagar was afraid when she and Ishmael were dying of thirst in the

---

4   See also Proverbs 9:10; Psalm 19:7–10; Psalm 25:14.

5   Genesis 3:10.

wilderness.[6] Jacob was afraid Laban would take his wives from him;[7] Jacob also was afraid his brother Esau might kill him for stealing Esau's inheritance.[8] Joseph's brothers were afraid when they were brought before him in Egypt.[9] Moses was afraid when he thought people might find out he had killed an Egyptian overseer.[10] The Hebrews were afraid when they saw fireworks on Mount Sinai[11] and when they saw Moses' shining face.[12] The boy Samuel was afraid to tell his vision to the priest Eli.[13] The Israelites were afraid of the Philistines.[14] Throughout 2 Samuel, 1 and 2 Kings, and 1 and 2 Chronicles, people were afraid of armies, enemies, and the consequences of their own bad behavior. The exiles returning to Judah were afraid of the occupying people who might try to stop them from rebuilding the Temple[15]. Mariners on the ship with Jonah were afraid all of them would sink because of him.[16]

In the New Testament, religious and political leaders were afraid of Jesus throughout his life; then they were afraid of his followers.[17] Shepherds were afraid when the angel appeared to them the night Jesus was born.[18] Believers and followers of Jesus were afraid of what might happen to them because they followed him.[19] Disciples were afraid of the crowds he attracted;[20] afraid when they found themselves on a boat in the middle of a storm;[21] afraid when they saw him walking on

---

[6]   Genesis 21:16.

[7]   Genesis 31:31.

[8]   Genesis 32:7, 11.

[9]   Genesis 43:18.

[10]   Exodus 2:14.

[11]   Exodus 20:18.

[12]   Exodus 34:30.

[13]   1 Samuel 3:15.

[14]   1 Samuel 7:7; 17:11, 24.

[15]   Ezra 4:4.

[16]   Jonah 1:4-6

[17]   Mark 11:18; Luke 22:2; Acts 16:35-38.

[18]   Luke 2:8-10.

[19]   Luke 5:8-11; John 9:22; Acts 5:17-42.

[20]   Matthew 14:15-17

[21]   Matthew 8:23-27; Mark 4:35-41; Luke 8:22-25.

water;[22] and they were afraid after he cast out demons,[23] when he talked about dying,[24] at the transfiguration,[25] and after the resurrection.[26] In Mark's Gospel, the women who were asked to "go tell" that the tomb was empty ran away and said nothing because they were afraid.[27]

Yes, fear is a useful emotion that can alert us to danger. But God does not mean for us to live in fear, to be paralyzed by fear, or to be motivated by fear.[28] In the grip of fear and anxiety, we do not make good choices. God always wants what is good for us and responds to our fear with words of assurance:

> **To Hagar:** *"What troubles you, Hagar? Do not be afraid; for God has heard the voice of the boy where he is. Come, lift up the boy and hold him fast with your hand, for I will make a great nation of him." Then God opened her eyes and she saw a well of water.* (Genesis 21:17–19)

> **To Jacob:** *"I am God, the God of your father; do not be afraid to go down to Egypt, for I will make of you a great nation there. I myself will go down with you to Egypt, and I will also bring you up again."* (Genesis 46:3–4)

> **Moses speaking God's assurance to the Hebrews:** *"Do not be afraid, stand firm, and see the deliverance that the LORD will accomplish for you today."* (Exodus 14:13)

---

22   Matthew 14:22-23; Mark 6:45-52; John 6:15-21.
23   Matthew 8:28-9:1; Mark 5:1-20; Luke 8:26-37
24   Matthew 17:22-23; Mark 9:30-32 10:32-33; Luke 9:43b-45.
25   Matthew 17:1-6; Mark 9:2-8; Luke 9:28-36.
26   Luke 24:36-37
27   Mark 16:8.
28   Psalm 91:5-12.

To Israel through the prophet Isaiah:[29] *"Do not fear, for I have redeemed you; I have called you by name, you are mine. When you pass through the waters, I will be with you; and through the rivers, they shall not overwhelm you; when you walk through fire you shall not be burned, and the flame shall not consume you. For I am the LORD your God, the Holy One of Israel, your Savior."* (Isaiah 43:1–3)

The angel to Mary: *"Do not be afraid, Mary, for you have found favor with God."* (Luke 1:30)

The angel to the shepherds: *"Do not be afraid; for see—I am bringing you good news of great joy for all the people: to you is born this day in the city of David a Savior, who is the Messiah, the Lord."* (Luke 2:10–11)

Jesus, when he called the disciples: *"Do not be afraid; from now on you will be catching people."* *When they had brought their boats to shore, they left everything and followed him.* (Luke 5:10–11)

Jesus to the disciples during the storm: *"Why are you afraid, you of little faith?" Then he got up and rebuked the winds and the sea; and there was a dead calm.* (Matthew 8:26)

But when they saw him walking on the sea, they thought it was a ghost and cried out; for they all saw him and were terrified. But immediately he

---

[29]   See also Isaiah 41:10–13; 51:12–13.

spoke to them and said, "Take heart, it is I; do not be afraid." (Mark 6:49–50)

On resurrection morning: *But the angel said to the women, "Do not be afraid; I know that you are looking for Jesus who was crucified. He is not here; for he has been raised, as he said."* (Matthew 28:5)

Jesus teaches us how to find freedom from fear.

As he walked through towns and cities where people existed with scarce resources and the oppression of an occupying army, Jesus taught them how to become free from the fear and anxiety that gripped their everyday lives. He taught them that the antidote for fear is faith:

> *And do not keep striving for what you are to eat and what you are to drink, and do not keep worrying. For it is the nations of the world that strive after all these things, and your Father knows that you need them. Instead, strive for his kingdom, and these things will be given to you as well. Do not be afraid, little flock, for it is your Father's good pleasure to give you the kingdom.* (Luke 12:29–32)

But, where do we, who live in a world filled with uncertainty and terror, find the confidence and strength not to be afraid, especially with our 24-7 news cycle that seems to intensify reasons to be afraid by repeating violent stories and pictures over and over? And since fear also may fill voting booths, there is a great incentive for political leaders to keep the stories coming. Campaign rallies and speeches by elected officials seem to focus more and more on what—and who—is threatening our very existence. Using fear this way is especially effective when it encourages voters to accept these messages without question because the fear has become so big and so uncomfortable we just don't want to be afraid anymore. Turning everything over to someone else is a strong impulse when we are caught up in unrelenting fear and anxiety. But is it the best choice? Remember, we don't make good decisions in the grip of fear. And that's exactly what people depend on when they encourage us to be afraid. Trouble is, *when we live in fear, we are not living in faith.*

So whom do we trust?

Through the ages, human beings have faced difficult and frightening times. And although we may ask why and how long, the real question has always been, Whom do we trust to lead us through valleys of fear? The answer was, and still is, God. Yes, we elect leaders and expect them to work together for the good of the people (*which is hard to define when so many people have such different ideas about what is good for the people*). But for Christians, our ultimate trust is in God. The Hebrew word we translate as "faith" means "trust." We often think of faith as believing, and it does mean that. But ultimately, faith means trusting that God's purposes are being worked out even when things aren't going the way we wish they would or think they should. Faith is trusting God even when we are afraid.

When we find ourselves gripped by fear, remember that these are not the only perilous times in human history; and by God's care and protection, humanity is still here. First-century Palestine was a grim place, where God's people lived in deep poverty under the boot of an occupying army. Roads often were lined with crosses where people died at the whim of a state that could cause a very pregnant young woman to make a dangerous journey for the sake of taking a census. Into this place, where hope seemed lost, God came softly and wonderfully to live among us and show us how love acts. And the world was forever changed.

When the news is filled with more floods, more fires, more people driven from their homes, another shooting, another bomb, a new disease, reports of the nations in an uproar, and the economy teetering again, it is very tempting to pull the covers over our heads and hope someone—anyone—will fix everything. Of course, there is a better way: to trust that the God who made the world is already at work in the world.[30]

> *God is our refuge and strength, a very present help in trouble. Therefore, we will not fear, though the earth should change, though the mountains shake in the heart of the sea; though its waters roar and foam, though the mountains tremble with its tumult. The nations are in an uproar, the kingdoms totter. The LORD of hosts is with us; the God of Jacob is our refuge. (Psalm 46:1–3, 6–7)*

> *For you did not receive a spirit of slavery to fall back into fear, but you have received a spirit of adoption. I consider that the sufferings of this present time are not worth comparing with the glory about to be revealed to us. We know that all things work together for good for those who love God, who are called according to his purpose.* (Romans 8:15, 18, 28)

---

[30]   Read more about overcoming fear: Psalm 27:1–3; 103:13–18; 118:6–9; Proverbs 3:24–26; 29:25; Isaiah 12:2; Matthew 10:31; 14:27; Luke 12:28–32; Hebrews 13:6; Revelation 1:17–18.

How do we move from fear to faith?

It's one thing to read, "Do not be afraid," and something entirely different to move beyond fear to claim the kind of faith that is built on trusting God. Peter Marshall, when he was chaplain of the US Senate, once said,

> To doubt either God's power, or God's love in our daily lives is to say by our actions: "Lord, I do not believe your promises. I do not think they really apply to me. I do not think You will do them. It might have been all right for Palestine in the long ago, but Lord, you just don't know Washington."[31]

Of course, God *does* know Washington and economics and geopolitics and the stock market and the allure of wealth and the intoxication of power and the dread of unexpected violence and what it is to be homeless and the sting of unjust accusers and the fear of being alone and abandoned. And God know us.

The remarkable thing is this: God didn't give up on Abraham or Hagar or Jacob or Moses or Joseph or the disciples when they didn't understand or the women at the tomb when they were afraid or Saul when he persecuted Christians or any of the other people God has used—and continues to use—to achieve Divine purposes. And God doesn't give up on us, but seeks us out and shows us how to believe and trust and love and forgive by doing it first—not because we are worthy, but because God wants us and promises to be with us, even in the valleys of fear.

---

[31]   Catherine Marshall, *A Man Called Peter:The Story of Peter Marshall*, (New York, New York: McGraw-Hill, 1951). p. 299.

Summary: Fear is a helpful feeling that can alert us to danger. But God does not mean for us to live in fear, to be paralyzed by fear, or even to be motivated by fear. In the grip of fear and anxiety, we do not make good choices, either as individuals or as a nation. When we move beyond the powerful and debilitating emotions of fear and anxiety, we can think more clearly and find reasonable, long-term solutions to the problems that cause us to be afraid. For Christians, the antidote for fear is faith— trusting in that wonderful assurance, *"Do not be afraid,"* because we know that God is big enough and strong enough and good enough and loving enough to use everything (*even our mistakes*) for good. Think about it, if the women who witnessed the resurrection had not been able to overcome their fear, how would we know about it today?

Jesus has the last word:

> *Peace I leave with you; my peace I give to you. I do not give to you as the world gives. Do not let your hearts be troubled, and do not let them be afraid.* (John 14:27)

Chapter 2

God and Anger

Do not be quick to anger, for anger lodges in
the bosom of fools. Do not say, "Why were
the former days better than these?" For it
is not from wisdom that you ask this.

—Ecclesiastes 7:9–10

It seems difficult, if not impossible, for people to talk about political differences without slipping into anger. And expressing anger in raw, unfiltered, and hurtful words has become the new normal. The rule of bullies in the playground has replaced "Miss Manners." So what's wrong with that? It feels honest. It feels strong. It feels good! Unless, of course, you're on the receiving end of anger. Unfortunately, in sustained and uncontrolled doses, anger can be a toxic emotion for those who give it and for those who receive it—flooding our stomachs with acid, our heads with ache, and our bodies with chemicals that add to heart, circulatory, and respiratory problems, not to mention ruining many Thanksgiving dinners, ending important friendships, and sometimes escalating into violence.

Fear and anger often are related, since unresolved fear can lead to becoming angry with the person, event, or idea that arouses fear. However, while fear can *paralyze* us, anger can *mobilize* us in ways that result in long-term consequences for the person who is angry and for unsuspecting and innocent people who become "collateral damage." Anger turned inward can become depression; anger turned outward can become aggression—emotional, verbal, or physical aggression. Like fear, there are some times when anger can be helpful and other times when it is toxic. Consider these three ways of understanding anger:

Anger Part 1: The Anger We Feel against Injustice

Many of us have heard a story—or seen a movie—about a person or group of people who are being used or abused by someone who is more powerful. And we have felt angry on behalf of those who are mistreated. Scripture offers good examples of this kind of anger.

In 2 Samuel 12:1–16, the prophet Nathan had to confront King David about his sin of having Uriah the Hittite killed in battle so David could marry Uriah's wife, Bathsheba. Rather than confront David outright, Nathan told the king a story: A rich man with many flocks needed to entertain a traveler, but he didn't want to kill one of his own sheep for the feast. So he stole a poor man's only lamb—a beloved family pet.

The injustice in this story made David so angry he said, "As the Lord lives, the man who has done this deserves to die."[32] Then Nathan replied, also in anger, "You. You are the man!"[33] What had been done in the story and in real life was wrong. Both saw an injustice: Nathan, in what David had done to Uriah; and David, in what the rich man in Nathan's story had done to the poor man. And both were angry on behalf of the one who had been wronged. However, they did not stay locked in anger. David and Nathan accepted God's resolution that showed more mercy for David than David was willing to offer the rich man in the story.[34] Anger was only *part of a process* that was followed by Divine justice, recognition of human responsibility, acceptance of God's will, and restoration of trust.[35]

At one time or another, Old Testament prophets showed anger on behalf of widows, orphans, the blind, the lame, the outcast, the outsider, and others who were taken advantage of by those who were more powerful.

Even Jesus showed anger in the face of injustice.

When the Pharisees plotted to have Jesus arrested for healing the man with a withered hand on the Sabbath, Mark's Gospel says, *"He looked around at them with anger; he was grieved at their hardness of heart and said to the man, 'Stretch out your hand.' He stretched it out, and his hand was restored."*[36]

---

[32]   2 Samuel 12:5.

[33]   2 Samuel 12:7.

[34]   2 Samuel 12:13.

[35]   2 Samuel 12:14–26.

[36]   Mark 3:5.

Of course, Jesus' most famous display of anger is the "temple tantrum," when he turned over tables and sent coins flying![37] Most of us were told that the cause of his anger was dishonest moneychangers and the people who sold animals to be sacrificed. But looking at Jesus' outburst through the eyes of all four Gospels, his anger seems to be about something more than that. Matthew, Mark, and John all report that he drives out *both* sellers *and* buyers; and in John's version, he even drives out the animals! So he must have been upset with something other than just the moneychangers and sellers.

Matthew goes on to say that Jesus did more than overthrow tables; he also challenged Temple rules by curing the blind and the lame (*who could not enter the Temple*) and welcoming children who sang "Hosanna"[38] (*which means "Save us, we pray!"*). In Luke's Gospel, he enters the Temple after weeping for Jerusalem and drives out the merchants to prepare for the teaching that follows in Luke 19:47 through 21:38. His anger, then, seems to be directed also at a Temple system that had become so lost in its own rules it excluded many of God's people from worship.

Anger serves a purpose only when we are able to let it go.

In both of these stories, anger was not Jesus' endgame but was part of a process that awakened those around him to the important message he was about to deliver. Anger had to give way to reason in order for the people to hear and understand what he was teaching. In the same way, *we* have to let go of anger in order to begin the rational, creative, and inspired thinking that produces real solutions.

Jesus' anger in the Temple captured people's attention and focused all parties on the radical change that was about to happen in the world because of him. But it was not anger that energized his ministry and

---

[37]   Matthew 21:12–17; Mark 11:15–19; Luke 19:45–48; John 2:13–22.

[38]   Matthew 21:14–15.

teaching. It was not anger that hovered over the final Passover meal with his followers. It was not anger that comforted him on the Mount of Olives. It was not anger that sustained him through his trial and crucifixion. It was not anger that allowed him to forgive the thief on the cross beside him and everyone else who was involved in his death. After the resurrection, it was not anger that helped him soothe his disciples' fears and doubts or that took him on the road to Emmaus[39] or that motivated him to prepare the breakfast by the lake.[40] It was not anger. It was love.

Anger against injustice is *part of a process* that lifts us up from outrage and frustration and then leads us into constructive and creative solutions to address injustice—a process that must eventually include forgiveness.

Anger Part 2: The Anger That Is Part of Grief

Anyone who has experienced an important loss also has experienced grief. And grief is not an event; it is a process. The stages of grief identified by the Swiss psychiatrist Elisabeth Kübler-Ross in her 1969 book, *On Death and Dying*, are the following:

Denial: This hasn't happened!

Anger: Why did this happen! Who is responsible?

Bargaining: What can I do to avoid or change this?

Depression: (*anger turned inward*)

Acceptance: It's going to be OK. I'm going to be OK.

As one who has experienced grief and walked with others on their journeys, I know that the path is not straight. We do not go from

---

[39]   Luke 24:13–31.
[40]   John 21:1–19.

denial, to anger, to bargaining, to depression, and to acceptance exactly in that order. It is normal to toggle back and forth from one stage to another or to be farther down the path and then return to one of the stages that has not been completed. But the process eventually should lead to acceptance, which is a new and healthy life. Unfortunately, it is possible *to become stuck* in one stage and not toggle back and forth or ever hope to move forward into the new reality that comes with acceptance. If the stage in which we become stuck is anger, it can consume all that we are or may become.

Although grief is most often associated with the death of someone we love, it can be part of any deeply felt loss, including the loss of relationships, jobs, health, home, neighborhood, sense of safety and security, lifestyle, social or economic status, upward mobility, hope for a better future, the way the world used to be, and the way we feel the world should be.

In recent election cycles, some of the anger we hear seems to be the result of individual and collective grief for a number of profound losses, such as the following:

- Middle-class economic prosperity that started slipping away when good-paying jobs were made obsolete by technology, while others were transferred to foreign countries

- Careers and savings that seemed to evaporate without warning in the banking crisis of 2008

- Lost hope for the future, especially for young people, in an economy they cannot influence or control

- Personal and national tragedies from ongoing wars that feel as if they have no end, that are fought by a few and ignored by many, and that seem to offer little possibility for what we traditionally have understood as "victory"

- The "television version" of the 1950s when life, as we remember it, was better, and people of different races and genders seemed to function in prescribed ways that felt "right" to those who didn't have to live with the indignity that others experienced

- In some regions of the country, the historic memory of the 1850s before the profound changes that came about during and after the American Civil War

Whether the grief process is personal, regional, or national, the problem of becoming stuck in anger has the same effect: being unable to go through the stages of grief and emerge on the other side with the vitality, health, and vision to create a new present and future.

Anger Part 3: "I'm mad as hell, and I'm not going to take it anymore."

The third—and most destructive—form of anger is the anger that says, "Things aren't going *my* way, and they should!" Most people can mutter or do something that eventually helps the feeling dissipate, and then it's over. When that doesn't happen (*when being angry feels more satisfying than not being angry*), there can be emotional outbursts that startle or upset those in the direct line of fire.

When anger becomes so deep-seated that we have trouble feeling any other way, it can result in depression (*when anger turns inward*) or aggression (*when anger turns outward*). The National Institutes of Health reports that unresolved and prolonged anger floods our bodies with chemicals that contribute to long-term health problems, such as high blood pressure, stroke, heart attack, vascular problems, bulimic behavior and other digestive disorders, type 2 diabetes, increased risk of highway accidents, teeth grinding, depression, anxiety, and skin conditions, to name just a few.[41]

---

[41]   See http://www.ncbi.nlm.nih.gov.

When unresolved anger is so ingrained that it becomes part of who we are, anger can nurse hatred: of individuals, of groups, of any institution that seems to be the reason the world is not behaving the way we think it should. This hatred can make some people susceptible to extreme ideas of religious, political, or cultural revenge—either individually or within a group of like-minded people. With enough emotional fuel, collective anger can lead to a mob mentality that results in the kinds of behavior individuals normally would not do on their own, including violence. Unfortunately, since collective anger is an effective way to generate poll numbers and media ratings, we probably can expect more emotional fuel from a number of sources.

The rule of law is one cultural counterbalance to collective anger. Another would be modeling our lives after the One who is called the Prince of Peace.

What does the Bible say about anger?

Interestingly, anger is the third emotion in the Genesis creation stories. The first is love (*God's love that brought creation into being*). The second is fear (*Adam and Eve's fear when they realized they could not hide their disobedience from God*). The consequences of the first two emotions were *life* (*from Divine creative love*) and *a changed relationship with God* (*from the fear that resulted from disobedience*). The third emotion—anger—set in motion the cascading events that led to the first murder. This was not just any murder, but was the murder of one family member by another family member.[42]

The story of Cain and Abel is so familiar it is easy to overlook the important lessons about anger and mercy that are hidden in the main plot: Cain, the firstborn son of Adam and Eve, is a farmer; and his younger brother, Abel, is a keeper of sheep. Cain decides to give some of his harvest as an offering to God, and Abel follows his older brother's

---

[42]   Genesis 4:1–16.

example by giving part of the firstlings of his flock. At this point, God has not asked for offerings, so why did Cain choose to make one? Was it out of gratitude for God's gift of good weather and soil? Or was it an effort to coax more good weather and soil from God for Cain's benefit?

Although Scripture is not clear about Cain's motive, we can guess that he probably was trying to encourage God to give him, Cain, what he needed to thrive. If Cain were giving purely out of gratitude, he would not have expected a *quid pro quo* from God. But he did expect something in return for his offering. Cain *wanted* God's favor, *expected* God's favor, and *felt entitled* to God's favor. When God preferred Abel's offering over his, Cain was furious!

Scripture doesn't give us a reason for God's preference. We don't need one. But in the conversation that follows Cain's angry outburst, we do learn that God cares about Cain and counsels him to master the sin of his jealousy and anger that is "lurking at the door."[43] But Cain defiantly holds on to his anger and allows it to fester and grow. Since he cannot lash back at God, Cain takes out his anger and jealousy on the brother whose offering was favored. Cain invites Abel to go into a field; and kills him. When God asks about Abel, Cain compounds his sins of anger and murder with dishonesty: "I do not know; am I my brother's keeper?"[44]

What happens next is not what we expect: God *could* do to Cain as Cain has done to Abel. God *could* kill Cain but chooses not to. Instead, God banishes Cain to a land east of Eden. His punishment is that he no longer will farm the land where his brother's blood cries out. Cain will be a fugitive and a wanderer. Both Cain and God know that "anyone who meets [Cain] may kill him,"[45] so God places a mark on him—not a mark of shame, but a mark of protection from those who

---

[43]   Genesis 4:7.

[44]   Genesis 4:9b.

[45]   Genesis 4:14.

would show less mercy than God already has shown by sparing and protecting Cain's life.

Here we see the great contrast between the Creator and human beings: the anger that seems so natural and satisfying to us is called sin by God. And the mercy that God so willingly offers by sparing Cain's life and marking him with Divine protection is alien to other human beings whose first impulse will be to give Cain the death penalty for killing his brother.

Of course, this is only the beginning.

There will be many times when anger raises its ugly head: Esau with Jacob,[46] Simeon and Levi,[47] Moses with Pharaoh,[48] Moses with the Hebrews in the wilderness,[49] Balaam with his donkey,[50] Balak with Balaam,[51] the general anger and violence of human against human that caused God to call for cities of refuge,[52] Samson's hot anger when his wife became the companion of his best man,[53] Eliab's anger against David for leaving the sheep to fight Goliath,[54] anger between Saul and Jonathan over David,[55] David's anger when Nathan condemns him for taking Bathsheba from her husband by killing him,[56] and King Ahasuerus' anger against Queen Vashti.[57]

---

[46] Genesis 27:43–45.
[47] Genesis 49:5–7.
[48] Exodus 11:8.
[49] Exodus 16:20–24; 32:19–22; Leviticus 10:16–17; Numbers 11:10–11; 16:16; 31:14–15.
[50] Numbers 22:27.
[51] Numbers 24:10.
[52] Deuteronomy 19:1–6.
[53] Judges 14:18–20.
[54] 1 Samuel 17:28.
[55] 1 Samuel 20:29–35.
[56] 2 Samuel 12:1–14.
[57] Esther 1:12–22.

What about God's anger?

God also becomes angry, especially as creation continues to ignore the will of the Creator. The Hebrews in the wilderness experience God's anger because of their constant complaining (*not to mention the Golden Calf incident*).[58] Then, as they prepare to cross the river into the Promised Land, Moses warns them that worshipping other gods surely will invoke the Lord's anger.[59] Of course, once they arrive, they forget everything Moses said and go back to their old ways.[60]

In spite of persistent human disobedience, Scripture tells us over and over that God's anger comes slowly and is modulated consistently with steadfast love, mercy, and forgiveness:[61]

> *The LORD is merciful and gracious, slow to anger and abounding in steadfast love. He will not always accuse, nor will he keep his anger forever. He does not deal with us according to our sins, nor repay us according to our iniquities. For as the heavens are high above the earth, so great is his steadfast love toward those who fear him; as far as the east is from the west, so far he removes our transgressions from us.* (Psalm 103:8–11)

---

[58] Numbers 11:1–2; 9–10; 12:6–10; 14:18–23; 22:21–27; 25:3–4; 32:10–14.

[59] Deuteronomy 4:1–2; 21–25; 6:15; 7:3–4; 11:17; 13:17; 29:18–20; 31:17–29; 32:20–22.

[60] Joshua 7:1;, 25–26; 23:16; Judges 2:11–21; 3:8–10; 10:6–8; 2 Samuel 6:6–7; 24:1–25; 1 Kings 14:9–15; 15:30; 16:1–3, 13, 26, 33; 21:22; 22:53; 2 Kings 3:3–5; 17:11–23; 21:6, 16; 22:17; 23:19–26; 1 Chronicles 13:10; 2 Chronicles 21:16; 28:25; 29:10; 30:8; 33:6; 34:25; Psalm 78:31–59; Jeremiah 7:18–20; 8:19; 11:17; 12:13; 15:14; 17:4; 21:5; 23:20; 25:6–7, 37–38; 32:31–32, 37; 42:18; 44:3–8.

[61] See also Exodus 34:5-6; Deuteronomy 9:19-21; Numbers 11:1-2; Judges 6:39-40; 1 Kings 3:3-15; Psalm 30:4-5; 78:21-25, 31-39; 85:1-4; 86:15; Isaiah 12:1-4; 54:9-10; 57:17-18; Micah 7:18-19; Zechariah 1:12-17; Hosea 14:1-7; Nehemiah 9:17.

When should human beings show anger toward each other?

The Psalms sometimes request (*or celebrate*) God's anger against the enemies of Israel.[62] However, both Psalms and Proverbs advise that human beings *should not* show anger toward each other:[63]

> *Fools show their anger at once, but the prudent ignore an insult.* (Proverbs 12:16)

> *Do not be quick to anger, for anger lodges in the bosom of fools. Do not say, "Why were the former days better than these?" For it is not from wisdom that you ask this.* (Ecclesiastes 7:9–10)

Just as God called Cain's anger and jealousy sin, Jesus also said that those who are angry and insult each other are subject to judgment:

> *You have heard that it was said to those of ancient times, "You shall not murder;" and "whoever murders shall be liable to judgment." But I say to you that if you are angry with a brother or sister, you will be liable to judgment; and if you insult a brother or sister, you will be liable to the council.* (Matthew 5:21–22)

The apostle Paul identified prolonged anger (*along with bitterness, abusive language, slander, and dishonesty*) as a threat to Christian witness and fellowship:

> *So then, putting away falsehood, let all of us speak the truth to our neighbors, for we are members of*

---

[62] Psalm 7:6; 76:7–9; 79:6–9.
[63] Read more about anger: Psalm 37:7–8; Proverbs 12:16; 14:29; 15:1, 18; 19:11; 16:32; 22:8–9, 24–25; 27:4; 29:11, 22; 2 Corinthians 12:20.

one another. . . . Put away from you all bitterness and wrath and anger and wrangling and slander, together with all malice, and be kind to one another, tenderhearted, forgiving one another, as God in Christ has forgiven you. (Ephesians 4:25, 31–32)

James also addressed anger in his letter:

You must understand this, my beloved: let everyone be quick to listen, slow to speak, slow to anger; for your anger does not produce God's righteousness. (James 1:19–20)

The antidote for anger is love and forgiveness.

Forgive others, forgive the situation in which you find yourself, forgive people you don't want to love or forgive, and forgive even your enemy (*yes, that's what Jesus said*).

Bear with one another and, if anyone has a complaint against another, forgive each other; just as the Lord has forgiven you, so you also must forgive. Above all, clothe yourselves with love, which binds everything together in perfect harmony. (Colossians 3:13)

Summary: Anger can be a useful emotion when it alerts us to injustice. Anger also is part of the grief process that takes us in stages from the loss of someone (*or something*) of great importance to the acceptance of a new reality. In either case, becoming stuck in anger is never useful. Letting go of anger is the first step toward the rational, creative, and inspired thinking that leads to effective answers to injustice. Moving beyond anger helps us emerge from grief with the health and vitality that make it possible to embrace a new life.

The third kind of anger—"I'm mad as hell, and I'm not going to take it anymore!"—comes from feelings that life is not happening the way we wish it would or think it should. Becoming stuck in this kind of anger can nurse hatred: of individuals, of groups, of any institution we think is the reason the world is not going our way. Hatred can make us susceptible to extreme ideas of religious, political, or cultural revenge—either individually or within a group of like-minded people. With enough emotional fuel, collective anger can lead to a mob mentality and encourage behavior—even violence—that individuals would not normally do on their own. Unresolved and prolonged anger of any kind floods our bodies with chemicals that often contribute to long-term health problems. Unfortunately, since collective anger is an effective way to generate poll numbers and media ratings, we probably can expect more emotional fuel from a number of sources.

Scripture tells us that anger is a sin. And the malice, bitterness, abusive language, slander, and dishonesty that grow out of anger threaten Christian witness and fellowship. Jesus says that anger and insulting behavior make us liable to judgment in the same way that murder does.[64] By his life and death, he teaches that the way we move beyond anger is through love and forgiveness—even for the enemy.

Jesus has the last word(s):[65]

> For if you forgive others their trespasses, your heavenly Father will also forgive you; but if you do

---

[64]   Matthew 5:21–24.

[65]   See also John 13:34–35; 14:15, 21; 15:9–12; Matthew 18:33–35; Mark 11:25; Luke 6:27–37.

not forgive others, neither will your Father forgive your trespasses. (Matthew 6:14–15)

Then Jesus said [from the cross], "Father, forgive them; for they do not know what they are doing." (Luke 23:34)

Chapter 3

God and Wealth (*and Poverty*)
Learning from the Past

When it comes to wealth and poverty in Scripture, there is one overarching, indisputable idea on which everything else rests: people do not create their own wealth all by themselves; it comes from God.

How wealth and poverty are understood among those who govern (*along with those who elect them and the journalists who write and talk about them*) often depends on where we find ourselves across the political spectrum. When the Right looks to the Left, they see the influence of community organizer Saul Alinsky, whose 1971 book, *Rules for Radicals*, focused on redistributing wealth and power to benefit the poor, especially African-Americans. The son of Russian Jewish immigrants, Alinsky said that when asked about religion, he always claimed his Jewish heritage. He also said he was agnostic.

When the Left looks to the Right, they see the influence of Ayn Rand, the Russian-born American novelist, philosopher, playwright, and screenwriter whose novel, *Atlas Shrugged*, has been recommended reading for some Republican staffers because of its emphasis on *laissez-faire* capitalism. Rand was an atheist who rejected God, religion, and altruism in favor of rational self-interest and a morality based on self-reverence and the pursuit of individual happiness in a world of "creators" and "haters."[66]

As political candidates and officeholders engage each other in a battle of the Russian-born atheist versus the Russian offspring agnostic, those of us who claim to be Christian may choose to look elsewhere for information—the Bible.

What *does* the Bible say about wealth and poverty?

The verse quoted most often these past few years in the halls of Congress has been consistent with Ayn Rand's celebration of individual success and rejection of altruism: *"Anyone unwilling to work should not eat."* (2 Thessalonians 3:9b)

---

[66] Ayn Rand, *Atlas Shrugged* (New York, New York: Signet, 1996). From her notes for *Atlas Shrugged* discussed in the introduction by Leonard Peikoff, pp. 1–8.

However, taking part of a verse out of context can be tricky, especially with the apostle Paul. As Paul went about spreading the Gospel among Gentiles, he would start a new church; then he would move on to plant another congregation or visit one he had established earlier. He kept in touch with them through letters that encouraged the new Christians *and* addressed problems that had come up in his absence. One especially frustrating problem was the interference of itinerate self-styled "apostles" who came in after Paul had moved on, and whose messages (*make that heresies*) were inconsistent with his understanding of the Gospel. Paul was not aware that his letters would become the books we read in the Bible. In almost all cases, he was addressing specific issues within a specific congregation, not developing a comprehensive theology. When all of Paul's letters are read as a whole, individual verses that fit one situation do not necessarily represent his views in other situations.

In Thessalonica, false preachers, perhaps using a bogus letter from Paul, seem to have convinced people that the second coming was imminent; and some of the members have quit working in order to prepare themselves.[67] Worse yet, they have become busybodies, probably encouraging others to follow their example. Paul was understandably upset.

However, 2 Thessalonians 3:9b does not represent all that Paul wrote about individual responsibility and Christian charity. One of his important projects was to collect an offering from Gentile congregations

---

[67]   **2 Thessalonians 2:1–5,** *"As to the coming of our Lord Jesus Christ and our being gathered together to him, we beg you, brothers and sisters, not to be quickly shaken in mind or alarmed, either by spirit or by word or by letter, as though from us, to the effect that the day of the Lord is already here. Let no one deceive you in any way; for that day will not come unless the rebellion comes first and the lawless one[j] is revealed, the one destined for destruction. He opposes and exalts himself above every so-called god or object of worship, so that he takes his seat in the temple of God, declaring himself to be God. Do you not remember that I told you these things when I was still with you?"*

on behalf of the Christians (*the saints*) in Jerusalem.[68] His "marks of the true Christian" include: *"Contribute to the needs of the saints,"* and *"If your enemies are hungry, give them food; if they are thirsty, give them something to drink."*[69] He also wrote, "[Peter and James] *asked only one thing, that we remember the poor, which was actually what I was eager to do."*[70]

Hovering over everything we read in the New Testament is Jesus of Nazareth. He did not work (*as Paul was quick to boast about doing*) but left his trade as a carpenter and called twelve others to leave their families and livelihoods to live in homeless poverty,[71] depending on the hospitality and benevolence of others.[72]

Understanding wealth and poverty begins with a deep dive into the Old Testament.

Most people in ancient Israel did not think of an afterlife the same way many of us do today. Generally, Sheol was understood as a place where the dead went regardless of their behavior while they were on earth (*although this thinking would evolve over time*). So for ancient Israel, rewards and punishment came in this world, not the next. Wealth often was seen as a sign of God's blessing, just as illness and misfortune were signs of punishment for sin.

Abraham and Sarah were promised (*and eventually received*) land, livestock, and offspring after they followed God "to a place I will show you."[73] (*Of course, along the way they managed to acquire additional*

---

68   See Romans 15:14–16; 25–32; 1 Corinthians 16:1–5; 2 Corinthians 8:1–8,; 9:1–15.
69   Romans 12:9–21; 15:25–27.
70   Galatians 2:9–10. See also 2 Corinthians 9:8–10.
71   Luke 9:57–58. See also Matthew 8:18–20.
72   Luke 8:1–3; 10:38–42.
73   Genesis 12:1–9.

land, livestock, and offspring by their own devices on the off chance that God had forgotten the promise.) Moses' final blessings for the Israelites as they prepared to cross into the Promised Land included the defeat of enemies, overflowing barns, and *"prosperity, in the fruit of your womb, in the fruit of your livestock, and in the fruit of your ground."*[74] Solomon was blessed with *"riches, possessions, and honor, such as none of the kings had"* because he asked only for wisdom and knowledge.[75]

However, the Old Testament concept of wealth isn't always that simple. Even then, God was not a Divine gumball machine where people put in a prayer or a good deed and out came the desires of their hearts. Good people experienced tragedies and losses[76] (*"Consider my servant Job"*), and bad people became powerful and wealthy—if only for a time.[77] In Proverbs, there is a connection between wealth and poverty and the way people live their lives. At the same time, Proverbs encourages us to look after the poor and warns against acquiring wealth at their expense:[78]

> *The wealth of the rich is their fortress; the poverty of the poor is their ruin.* (Proverbs 10:15)

> *Whoever is kind to the poor lends to the LORD, and will be repaid in full.* (Proverbs 19:17)

---

[74] Deuteronomy 28:1–14.

[75] 2 Chronicles 1:12.

[76] Job 5:5–7 *"The hungry eat their harvest, and they take it even out of the thorns; and the thirsty pant after their wealth. For misery does not come from the earth, nor does trouble sprout from the ground; but human beings are born to trouble just as sparks fly upward."*

[77] Job 20:4–5, 10–11 *"Do you not know this from of old, ever since mortals were placed on earth, that the exulting of the wicked is short, and the joy of the godless is but for a moment? Their children will seek the favor of the poor, and their hands will give back their wealth. Their bodies, once full of youth, will lie down in the dust with them."*

[78] See also Proverbs 17:5; 21:13; 22:2–9; 31:8–9.

Oppressing the poor in order to enrich oneself, and giving to the rich, will lead only to loss. (Proverbs 22:16)

Wealth also was part of the spoils of war that could go either way—depending on which group God blessed with victory or disciplined with defeat:[79]

Your wealth and all your treasures I will give for spoil as the price of your sin throughout all your territory. By your own act you shall lose the heritage that I gave you, and I will make you serve your enemies in a land that you do not know. Thus says the LORD: Cursed are those who trust in mere mortals and make mere flesh their strength. (Jeremiah 17:3b–5)

When it comes to wealth and poverty in Scripture, there is *one overarching, indisputable idea* on which everything else rests: people do not create their own wealth all on their own; it comes from God.

Do not say to yourself, "My power and the might of my own hand have gotten me this wealth." But remember the LORD your God, for it is he who gives you power to get wealth. (Deuteronomy 8:17–18a)

In fact, too much human arrogance in this matter can lead to trouble:

By your wisdom and your understanding you have amassed wealth for yourself, and have gathered

---

[79]   See also Jeremiah 15:13; 20:5; Hosea 12:8–9; Habakkuk 2:7–14; Zephaniah 1:12–13.

gold and silver into your treasuries. By your great
wisdom in trade you have increased your wealth,
and your heart has become proud in your wealth.
Therefore thus says the Lord GOD: "Because
you compare your mind with the mind of a god,
therefore, I will bring strangers against you, the
most terrible of the nations; they shall draw their
swords against the beauty of your wisdom and
defile your splendor." (Ezekiel 28:4–7)

What does this mean for us in the twenty-first century?

In today's financial world of stocks, derivatives, and other nontangible wealth, it can be difficult for us to see a connection between *our* understanding of wealth and the biblical idea of "prosperity from field, flock, and family" that comes from God. It seems almost un-American to think that what we have (*what we have built and acquired and earned*) somehow is not something we can take credit for all on our own. It is much easier for us to see a world that *we* make; and in that world, the idea of charity for the needs of others strikes many as quaint and unnecessary since the "others" many of us know often are people like us who don't need charity.

And yet if we believe in a Creator God and a Redeemer Son, we are drawn into a reality of shared existence where wealth does not exist without poverty; and poverty does not exist without wealth. This is the world that Scripture addresses: a world in which God presents us with a moral obligation *not* to keep all the riches we think we earned. In this world, we are instructed (*by God*) to give a tithe from the "first fruits" of our wealth to support worship.[80] In this world, we are commanded (*by God*) to protect the well-being of the community both directly (*by helping the least and most vulnerable*) and indirectly

---

[80]   See Exodus 23:16–19; Leviticus 2:14; 23:10–20; Deuteronomy 18:3–4; 2 Chronicles 31: 4–7.

(*in the social, business, and legal practices that impact the community*).[81] Through the Moral Holiness Code,[82] God explains our moral and ethical responsibilities to each other and to the community in practical instructions for neighborliness, charity, business, agriculture, family life, and civic responsibilities:

> *When you reap the harvest of your land, you shall not reap to the very edges of your field, or gather the gleanings of your harvest. You shall not strip your vineyard bare, or gather the fallen grapes of your vineyard; you shall leave them for the poor and the alien: I am the LORD your God.*

> *You shall not steal; you shall not deal falsely; and you shall not lie to one another. And you shall not swear falsely by my name, profaning the name of your God: I am the LORD.*

> *You shall not defraud your neighbor;[83] you shall not steal; and you shall not keep for yourself the wages of a laborer until morning.[84] You shall not revile the deaf or put a stumbling block before the blind; you shall fear your God: I am the LORD.*

---

81   See also Isaiah 58:1–14; Micah 3:1–12.

82   Leviticus 19:1–37.

83   In Luke 10:25–37, Jesus identified who "the neighbor" is by answering the young lawyer's question, "Who is my neighbor?" with the story of the Good Samaritan. Since Jews and Samaritans had been natural enemies for over seven hundred years, when Jesus described a Samaritan as a good neighbor, he was saying, "The neighbor is everyone else, including the enemy."

84   See also Deuteronomy 24:14–15 *"You shall not withhold the wages of poor and needy laborers, whether other Israelites or aliens who reside in your land in one of your towns. You shall pay them their wages daily before sunset because they are poor and their livelihood depends on them."*

You shall not render an unjust judgment; you shall not be partial to the poor or defer to the great: with justice you shall judge your neighbor. You shall not go around as a slanderer among your people, and you shall not profit by the blood of your neighbor: I am the LORD.

You shall not hate in your heart; you shall not criticize your neighbor. You shall not take vengeance or bear a grudge, but you shall love your neighbor as yourself: I am the LORD.

You shall rise before the aged, and defer to the old; and you shall fear your God: I am the LORD.

When an alien resides with you in your land, you shall not oppress the alien. The alien who resides with you shall be to you as the citizen among you; you shall love the alien as yourself, for you were aliens in the land of Egypt: I am the LORD your God.

You shall not cheat in measuring length, weight, or quantity. You shall have honest balances, honest weights, an honest [measure of grain], and an honest [liquid measure]: I am the LORD your God, who brought you out of the land of Egypt.

The Sabbatical Year was an economical and ecological "reboot."

The sabbatical year[85] was commanded by God to give rest to the earth—and to the created life on the earth—every seventh year. It also

---

[85]   Deuteronomy 15:1–23.

contained a redistribution of wealth since debts would be forgiven and slaves would be set free with liberal provisions from the slave owner's flock, threshing floor, and wine press. Even the firstling ox would be exempt from work, and the firstling sheep would not be shorn.[86] God anticipated that people might try to find loopholes and added:

> *If there is among you anyone in need . . . do not be hard-hearted or tight-fisted toward your needy neighbor. You should rather open your hand, willingly lending enough to meet the need, whatever it may be. Be careful that you do not entertain a mean thought, thinking, "The seventh year, the year of remission, is near," and therefore view your needy neighbor with hostility and give nothing. . . . Give liberally and be ungrudging when you do so [and] the LORD your God will bless you in all that you undertake. Since there will never cease to be some in need on the earth, I therefore command you, "Open your hand to the poor and needy in your land."* (Deuteronomy 15:7–11)

Did Israel always follow these commandments? Of course not! Scripture points to excesses of wealth and power among the few at the expense of the many, especially injustice "in the gate."[87] The city gate was where men of wealth and influence gathered to conduct business, dispense justice, and hear the complaints of the poor. The husband

---

[86]   Seven sabbatical years (7 × 7 = 49 years) would usher in the Jubilee on the fiftieth year, when "you shall proclaim liberty throughout the land to all its inhabitants." Property would revert to its original owners, and people would not labor but would "eat only what the field itself produces." Requirements for the Jubilee, found in Leviticus 25:10–18, include the ethics of "not cheating your neighbor" in buying and selling land.

[87]   See also Isaiah 29:18–21; Amos 5:7–15; Proverbs 22:21–25.

of the good wife in Proverbs[88] was one of the men sitting "in the gate" while she managed the household, provided food for the servants, assessed and bought land, planted a vineyard, ran a profitable business making and selling linen garments, and raised their children. "The gate" was a combination courthouse, financial district, civic club, and smoke-filled back room where political and economic power was created and exercised. And like most places of power, the city gate became, for some, a breeding ground for corruption and greed.[89]

> *The people of the land have practiced extortion and committed robbery; they have oppressed the poor and needy, and have extorted from the alien without redress.* (Ezekiel 22:29)

Injustice "in the gate" had unintended consequences.

Ironically, the gate also was a place where the city was vulnerable to enemy invasion. Injustice "in the gate" added to the problem because it tore at the fabric of community and made them less able to come together in defense.

> *Ah, you who make iniquitous decrees, who write oppressive statutes, to turn aside the needy from justice and to rob the poor of my people of their right, that widows may be your spoil, and that you may make the orphans your prey! What will you do on the day of punishment, in the calamity that will come from far away? To whom will you flee for help, and where will you leave your wealth, so as not to crouch among the prisoners or fall among the slain.* (Isaiah 10:1–4)

---

[88] Proverbs 31.

[89] See also Job 5:3–7; Proverbs 14:23; 22:22–23; Isaiah 29:20–21; Amos 5:11–15; 8:4–7.

Isaiah identified a similar threat in the countryside where wealthy landowners used inheritance laws, taxation, and predatory lending to take land from widows and foreclose on small farms, forcing many people into cities where they lived in poverty. These practices allowed the owners of big houses to acquire *lots* of land—with the unintended consequence that they also became isolated and vulnerable to marauding invaders.

> *Ah, you who join house to house, who add field to field, until there is room for no one but you, and you are left to live alone in the midst of the land! The LORD of hosts has sworn in my hearing: Surely many houses shall be desolate, large and beautiful houses, without inhabitant. . . . Then the lambs shall graze as in their pasture, fatlings and kids shall feed among the ruins. Ah, you who call evil good and good evil, who put darkness for light and light for darkness, who put bitter for sweet and sweet for bitter! Ah, you who are wise in your own eyes, and shrewd in your own sight! Ah, you . . . who acquit the guilty for a bribe, and deprive the innocent of their rights!* (Isaiah 5:8–24)

In time, partisan fighting and economic fractures in both kingdoms (*that once had been the Promised Land*) became an invitation for foreign armies to invade. The Northern Kingdom (*called Israel, Samaria, House of Joseph or Ephraim*) fell to Assyria in 722 BCE, and the population was scattered in a great Diaspora. The Southern Kingdom (*Judah*) was defeated, and the Temple was destroyed by Babylon in 586 BCE. Religious leaders, along those who had wealth, power, and education, were marched into exile in Babylon, while others were left behind to work for the foreigners who now occupied the land. When the first exiles returned in 538 BCE, they found bitter resentment among those who had remained, and aggressive hostility with the Samaritans[90] who occupied land that was previously the Northern Kingdom. Unable to heal old wounds and resolve ongoing political conflict, the area came under the domination of one foreign power after another.

Summary: For ancient Israel, rewards and punishment came in this life, not the next. Wealth often was seen as a sign of God's blessing, just as illness and misfortune were signs of punishment for sin. However, the Old Testament concept of wealth isn't always that simple. Good people experience tragedies and losses, and bad people become powerful and wealthy—if only for a time. In Scripture, the overarching, indisputable idea on which everything rests is this: people do not create wealth all on their own; it comes from God.

In today's financial world of stocks, derivatives, and other nontangible wealth, it can be difficult for us in the twenty-first century to see a connection between *our* understanding of wealth and the biblical idea of "prosperity from field, flock, and family" that comes from God. It seems almost un-American to think that what we have (*what we have built and acquired and earned*) somehow *is not something we can take credit for on our own.*

And yet if we believe in a Creator God and a Redeemer Son, we are drawn into a reality of shared existence where wealth does not exist without poverty; and poverty does not exist without wealth. This

---

[90] Scripture is unclear about who the Samaritans were. They could have been the offspring of marriages between Assyrian invaders and some of the Israelites who were not part of the Diaspora. They followed the teaching of Moses, and as we discover in Jesus' encounter with the Samaritan woman at the well, they worshipped the Hebrew God, but on a different mountain since the Temple had been destroyed. Samaritans and Jews were natural enemies for over seven hundred years when Jesus told the parable about the Good Samaritan, which would have been a scandal to any Jew because there was no such thing as a "good" Samaritan.

is the world that Scripture addresses: a world in which God presents us with a moral obligation *not* to keep all the riches we think we earned. In this world, we are instructed (*by God*) to protect the wellbeing of the community both directly (*by helping the least and most vulnerable*) and indirectly (*in the social, business, and legal practices that include fairness to workers*). Why? Because a healthy community is essential for the overall safety and survival of all people—both rich and poor.

Jesus has the last word:

> *When some were speaking about the temple, how it was adorned with beautiful stones and gifts dedicated to God, [Jesus] said, "As for these things that you see, the days will come when not one stone will be left upon another; all will be thrown down."* (Luke 21:5–6)

Chapter 4

God and Poverty

Although God Incarnate had all power to come in
the form of a military leader, as people expected the
Messiah would do, he chose not to. Nor did he come
as an emperor with great power or a king with great
wealth or a religious leader with great authority.
He chose, instead, to live among us in poverty.

But why? Why this choice?

In American politics, it is almost impossible for candidates, elected officials, and voters to avoid issues that have their roots in poverty. How we feel about these issues and how reporters and commentators write and speak about them have a lot to do with personal and cultural experiences. As Christians, we hold the current reality of poverty in one hand, while in the other hand we have the New Testament story about how the ancient understanding of wealth as a blessing and poverty as a curse was turned upside down by a child of lowly birth. Think about it. Although God Incarnate had all power to come in the form of a military leader, as people expected the Messiah would do, he chose not to. Nor did he come as an emperor with great power or a king with great wealth or a religious leader with great authority. He chose, instead, to come . . . well, you know how.

A seminary friend, who worked for a time monitoring the Israeli-Palestinian boarder, wrote one year just before Christmas: "After a recent visit to the northern West Bank, I finally understand the Nativity. We traveled there in the company of shepherds who led us to the place where they keep their sheep. It was a low, dark cave. Noisy, crowded with animals and smelling like, well, sheep dung. The mangers were rusty, with animals pushing at each other to find space to eat. Not the sort of place where you would want to give birth. If God can be born here, God can be born anywhere."

Yes, God *could* be born anywhere but chose, instead, to come among us and live in poverty.[91] And the great good news of this coming was announced, *not* to the rich and powerful or to religious authorities, but to shepherds who meant so little they didn't even have to leave their fields to be part of the census that had brought Mary and Joseph to Bethlehem. They literally didn't count. But why? Why this choice? Consider these possibilities:

---

[91]   See 2 Corinthians 8:9.

By coming in poverty, Jesus maintained continuity with what God had already said and done in the world.

Jesus' poverty does affirm, in a deeply personal way, the understanding that the God of power and might is also the protector of the poor and the afflicted, as we hear in Mary's song held side by side with Psalm 22 and in Jesus' words as they echo Old Testament messages:

Mary's Song (Luke 1:46–55)	**Psalm 22**
My soul magnifies the Lord, and my spirit rejoices in God my Savior, for he has looked with favor on the lowliness of his servant.	*You who fear the LORD, praise him!*
Surely, from now on all generations will call me blessed; for the Mighty One has done great things for me, and holy is his name.	*For he did not despise or abhor the affliction of the afflicted; he did not hide his face from me, but heard when I cried to him. From you comes my praise in the great congregation; my vows I will pay before those who fear him.*
His mercy is for those who fear him from generation to generation.	*The poor shall eat and be satisfied; those who seek him shall praise the LORD. May your hearts live forever!*
He has shown strength with his arm; he has scattered the proud in the thoughts of their hearts.	*All the ends of the earth shall remember and turn to the LORD; and all the families of the nations shall worship before him. For dominion belongs to the LORD, and he rules over the nations.*
He has brought down the powerful from their thrones, and lifted up the lowly; he has filled the hungry with good things, and sent the rich away empty.	*Posterity will serve him; future generations will be told about the Lord, and proclaim his deliverance to a people yet unborn, saying that he has done it.*
He has helped his servant Israel, in remembrance of his mercy, according to the promise he made to our ancestors, to Abraham and to his descendants forever.	

Isaiah 56:6–8

Is not this the [worship that I prefer]: to loose the bonds of injustice, to undo the thongs of the yoke, to let the oppressed go free, and to break every yoke?

Is it not to share your bread with the hungry, and bring the homeless poor into your house; when you see the naked, to cover them?

Then your light shall break forth like the dawn, and your healing shall spring up quickly; your vindicator shall go before you, the glory of the LORD shall be your rear guard.

Isaiah 41:18–18, 20

When the poor and needy seek water, and there is none, and their tongue is parched with thirst, I the LORD will answer them, I the God of Israel will not forsake them. I will open rivers on the bare heights, and fountains in the midst of the valleys; I will make the wilderness a Pool of water, and the dry land springs of water . . . so that all may see and know, all may consider and understand, that the hand of the Lord has done this, the Holy One of Israel has created it.

Matthew 25:35–36, 40

I was hungry and you gave me food,

I was thirsty and you gave me something to drink,

I was a stranger and you welcomed me,

I was naked and you gave me clothing,

I was sick and you took care of me,

I was in prison and you visited me.

Truly I tell you, just as you did it to one of the least of these, you did it to me.

John 4:13–14

Jesus said to [the Samaritan woman at the well], "Everyone who drinks of this water will be thirsty again, but those who drink of the water that I will give them will never be thirsty. The water that I will give will become in them a spring of water gushing up to eternal life."

Psalm 12:5	Luke 4:18–19
"Because the poor are despoiled, because the needy groan, I will now rise up," says the LORD; "I will place them in the safety for which they long."	*The Spirit of the Lord is upon me, because he has anointed me to bring good news to the poor. He has sent me to proclaim release to the captives and recovery of sight to the blind, to let the oppressed go free, to proclaim the year of the Lord's favor.*

Jesus became the "in-your-face" reality of what it means to be poor.

For all that has changed from the first century to the twenty-first century, the idea of looking directly into the human faces of systemic poverty is still something we avoid. In ancient Israel, people walked past the poor and disenfranchised as they begged in the streets, and created effective barriers to keep them out of the Temple. In many ways, we follow their example. Poverty is uncomfortable and disturbing when it comes too close, because it arouses powerful feelings of sympathy, cynicism, helplessness, shame, anger, judgment, impatience, arrogance, pity, resolve, compassion, irritation, fear, revulsion, confusion, hopelessness, respect, doubt (*you fill in the rest*). We would rather keep the poor invisible and someplace where we are not—geographically and emotionally. And like ancient Israel, on some level we need to believe that the poor are poor because of something they have done or not done. Otherwise, it (*poverty*) could happen to anyone—it could happen to us.

Trouble is, because God Incarnate chose to live among us in poverty, we are forced to look into the faces of poverty—if we are willing to see. We are forced even to love them—if we are willing to feel. And for those of us who claim to be Christians, Jesus' reality also carries expectations for how we *think* about, *talk* about, and *treat* those who are poor – in news stories and commentaries, in campaigning and governing, in discussions with family and friends, and in our own heads. This is not about political correctness. It's about biblical correctness.

Some people believe that when Jesus said, *"You always have the poor with you,"*[92] he was suggesting that the historical pervasiveness of poverty means it is here to stay. So we are under no moral obligation to find a better way for people to live. However, when we read this in the context of his life and teaching, it is more likely that he was recognizing the reality of human forces and conditions—up and down the economic ladder—that create and feed systemic poverty. The widow's small offering[93] was not the result of laziness or lack of initiative; it was about inheritance laws that threw widows and orphans into grim and brief lives. The begging leper who knelt before Jesus[94] was not trying to get something for nothing. He was suffering from a disease that cut him off from human contact. The blind beggar outside Jericho[95] could not overcome his situation by getting a job and working hard. His only hope was to accept humiliation and become a nuisance to the disciples and to everyone in the crowd so Jesus might notice him.

Jesus knew that poverty is *at least as much* about ignorance[96] as it is about idleness.

---

[92]   John 12:8a.

[93]   Luke 21:1–4. See also Mark 12:41–44.

[94]   Mark 1:40–42.

[95]   Luke 18:35–43.

[96]   **Before you overreact:** Ignorance does not mean being "stupid" or "inferior" or "inadequate." Ignorance simply means not having all the information available on a particular subject or idea. Perfectly intelligent and competent people can be ignorant about some matters because the information they have is incomplete, outdated, or incorrect. Being referred to as "ignorant" is not an insult. However, having access to legitimate information and choosing to ignore or dismiss it because it doesn't agree with current thinking is not ignorance. That's something else.

When confronted with a man born blind[97] (*who also was begging because what else could the blind or the lame or the sick or the outcast do?*), Jesus understood that everyone—the man's parents, the religious authorities, the crowds, even his disciples—believed the man's blindness must have been the result of sin, as was the shame and isolation and poverty that came with his blindness. He also knew that making mud on the Sabbath and putting it on the man's eyes would draw him— Jesus—into their debate. The question for them was, Who sinned? The man? His parents? Jesus? All of the above?

But for Jesus, the question was not about sin. It was about seeing—looking through the man's blind eyes and experiencing the world he experienced every day. It was about looking into the face of this man who had been born blind and seeing his humanity underneath layers of emotional and physical poverty that had resulted from the thoughts, words, and actions of the people around him from the day he was born. More importantly, it was about looking into the face of the man who had been born blind and seeing that he, too, was created in the image of God. Jesus knew this healing would be the revelation of God in their very midst. He was correcting their ignorance and giving sight—*enlightenment*—to everyone! Then the question became, Did they see? Well, the man born blind saw for the first time and worshipped Jesus. The Pharisees refused to see, declared Jesus a sinner, and drove the man away. The disciples weren't sure *what* they had seen.

What do we see when we see poverty?

Growing up in a small Appalachian town before the government declared war on poverty, I was unaware that the world I knew was not the world everywhere, except in books. There were a few families who lived in large homes and whose children attended school with everyone else. For the most part, the rest of us came from modest households

---

[97]   John 9:1-41.

with great hopes and expectations for their offspring. There were a few children who lived "up the hollers" where I had never been. They were pale, had rough hands, rarely smiled, wore the same clothes day after day, and carried themselves like exhausted adults. These children got to leave class midmorning to earn their lunches by working in the school kitchen, and they didn't return until later in the afternoon when all the dishes had been washed and dried and the lunchroom had been cleaned. They almost never had books or paper or pencils—something that visibly irritated our teachers. In the winter, they and their clothes smelled, and we would ask permission not to sit beside them.

One Sunday, while a friend and I were eating cookies between Sunday school and worship, we started to talk about a tall boy in our grade at school who obviously was older than we were and who had become particularly "ripe" during the winter. My father overheard and took me aside to suggest that I might consider being more kind and compassionate. He explained that not everyone had a warm house with indoor plumbing. Some people had to carry water from the nearest river or creek where they also bathed and washed clothes—very difficult to do in winter.

When this same boy found and kept a pair of eyeglasses that one of our classmates had carelessly left lying about, people wondered why he would steal something that could not possibly be of any use to him. He was expelled from school and sent to a place for young thieves. We never saw him again. To this day, I believe he was not a thief but acted out of complete poverty. He simply had nothing, not one thing, to call his own.

That is how I came to believe that poverty is (*at least partly*) the result of ignorance—the ignorance of children who do not have blocks or crayons to help them learn letters and colors, who do not have books or paper or pencils, who have only partial access to the public education we say we offer equally to all children, who do not have parents to make them study when they would rather play and go to bed when they would rather stay up, who do not have water that is clean and safe, who go to bed hungry and go to school hungry, who learn more about humiliation and violence than they do about history and grace, who grow into adulthood with the DNA of scarcity in their bones, who don't know the rules about getting and keeping a job because they don't know anyone who has a job. They do, however, know one thing well: the stigma and stench of poverty that they cannot wash off without help.

Poverty also results from the ignorance of people, such as I, who grew up believing that the world is kind and fair and generous to everyone—if only we try hard enough; who take for granted warm baths, regular meals, and a place to sleep that is safe and clean; who assume that all people have choices about how and where they live and work; who have lapses in basic math skills as we hear about parents working two or three jobs (*for little money and no benefits*) and somehow miss the reality that even if they work twenty-four hours a day, they cannot find a way out of poverty.

Since most political candidates, elected officials, media reporters, and commentators have achieved positions of wealth and prominence, it is safe to assume that they, too, know very little about the daily grind of hunger, humiliation, danger, and hopelessness that is the only reality for many people, including children.

Recognizing my part in the very complex issue of poverty does not lay the responsibility only at my feet, any more than it excuses those who are poor from doing their part. However, admitting that this *is* a complex issue, to which we all contribute in one way or another, may be the most honest and most Christian way to understand and address something that happens each day at a great price for all of us.

It costs us nothing to use language that calms emotions (*instead of inciting them*).

In fact, changing the tone and tenor of private conversations and public discourse *can* go a long way toward productive discussions about poverty. At the same time, it costs us nothing to treat people up and down the economic ladder with respect and dignity, and it makes all of us better human beings.

The recommendation to have compassion and to walk in the other person's shoes before judging them didn't come only from my father (*who, by the way, worked hard and expected the same from me*). I learned about compassion while sitting in church, even though church people, being the works in progress that we are, don't *always* demonstrate the same compassion that Jesus so generously gives to us. Mostly, I learned about compassion from what Jesus said and did. We, who call ourselves Christians, may want to consider his words as we talk about the poor in our own heads, among groups of people, in tweets and social media, and in political discourse:

Hear who is blessed . . .[98]

> *Blessed are you who are poor, for yours is the kingdom of God. Blessed are you who are hungry now, for you will be filled. Blessed are you who weep now, for you will laugh. Blessed are you when people hate you, and when they exclude you, revile you, and defame you on account of the Son of Man.* (Luke 6:20-22)

Hear whom we are supposed to love . . .[99]

> *Love your enemies, do good to those who hate you, bless those who curse you, pray for those who abuse you. If anyone strikes you on the cheek, offer the other also; and from anyone who takes away your coat do not withhold even your shirt. Give to everyone who begs from you; and if anyone takes away your goods,*

---

[98]   See also Matthew 5:1–12.

[99]   See also Matthew 5:43–45.

do not ask for them again. Do to others as you would
have them do to you. (Luke 6:27-31)

Understand there is no credit for doing what is easy . . .[100]

If you love those who love you, what credit is
that to you? For even sinners love those who love
them. If you do good to those who do good to you,
what credit is that to you? For even sinners do the
same. But love your enemies, do good, and lend,
expecting nothing in return. (Luke 6:32-35a)

Let God do the judging; it's not our job . . .[101]

Do not judge, and you will not be judged; do
not condemn, and you will not be condemned.
Forgive, and you will be forgiven; give, and it will
be given to you. (Luke 6:37-38a)

Summary: Jesus called the poor "blessed" because someone had to.
He pitched his tent with them because nobody else would. His choice
to live and teach among us in poverty forces us to look into the faces
of the poor and see the image of God. When we judge, reject, isolate,
exploit, and blame the poor, we deny the Divine image that is in them,
and we deny the image of God that also is in us.

Poverty cannot come about only because of idleness, since there
is an abundance of idleness among all of us, including those who
enjoy material wealth. Regardless of what causes poverty (*circumstance,*
condition, lack of initiative, public policies, social upheaval, ignorance, or
inheritance), it is maintained not only by wrong choices made by those

---

[100]   See also Matthew 5:46–48.
[101]   See also Matthew 7:1–5.

who are poor but also by the good intentions and thoughtless denials of those who enjoy various levels of material wealth, including me.

Recognizing that we, individually and collectively, have a part in the very complex issue of poverty does not lay the responsibility only at our feet, any more than it excuses those who are poor from doing their part. However, admitting that this *is* a complex issue, to which we all contribute in one way or another, may be the most honest and most Christian way to understand and address something that happens each day at a great price for all of us.

It costs us nothing to use language that calms emotions about this hot-button issue, and it can go a long way toward productive discussions. It costs us nothing to treat people up and down the economic ladder with respect and dignity, and it makes all of us better human beings.

In his life and ministry, Jesus looks at us with the face of poverty and challenges us to see that each of us shares life from the same Source. He says to us that God's abundance has been given to all of us, and that from those of us who have so much, much compassion and generosity are expected. Then he shows us what compassion and generosity look like by doing it first—on the cross.

Jesus has the last word:

> *For I was hungry and you gave me food, I was thirsty and you gave me something to drink, I was a stranger and you welcomed me, I was naked and you gave me clothing, I was sick and you took care of me, I was in prison and you visited me. . . . Truly I tell you, just as you did it to one of the least of these, you did it to me.* (Matthew 25:35–40)

Chapter 5

God and Wealth

By choosing to live among us as one of the homeless poor, Jesus redefined wealth.

Even though Old Testament concepts of wealth and poverty are more complex than the simple equations that wealth is good and poverty is bad, that generally is how human beings have understood the paradigm for thousands of years. Therefore, it seems appropriate for those who *have* wealth to use the political, social, and economic systems available to them to *increase* their wealth with little regard for the impact on those who have less. After all, don't *they* have the same opportunities everyone else has? There is nothing legally wrong with this idea. However, for those of us who claim to be Christians, there is an added dimension that complicates all these straightforward equations. Along came a Rich Man who asked Jesus how he could inherit eternal life.[102]

By all standards, this Rich Man also was a good man who had followed, all his life, the commandments brought down from the mountain by Moses. His question to Jesus was simple: "Is there anything else I should do?"

> *Jesus, looking at him, loved him and said, "You lack one thing; go, sell what you own, and give the money to the poor and you will have treasure in heaven; then come and follow me."* [The man] *went away grieving, for he had many possessions.* (Mark 10:21–22)

I have known this story nearly all my life, but have never heard anyone (*apart from a few monks*) suggest that Jesus really meant we should sell all we have and give the money to the poor. Perhaps a faithful tithe to the church, but not everything and not directly to the poor. Trouble is, those *are* the words he used. Of course, if that happened, the poor would become rich, and they would just have to sell everything they had and give the money back to those who had been rich but were

---

102 See the story of the Rich Man in Mark 10:17–22. In Matthew 19:16–22, he is called a Rich Young Man. In Luke 18:18–24, he is the Rich Ruler.

now poor. This kind of circular redistribution of money and things wouldn't solve the real problem of wealth, as Jesus seemed to see it, even though everyone *would* have an opportunity to experience both wealth and the problem of wealth at one time or another.

Interestingly, many preachers are reluctant to talk about money in sermons, unless they have big operations to support that require constant infusions of cash. And yet it was a frequent topic for Jesus. Of course, what he says about money is complicated, and most of us tend to filter his preaching and parables through our own ideas about how we see the world and how we want it to be—for us. For instance, it is easy to read, *"Ask, and it will be given you; search, and you will find; knock, and the door will be opened for you."*[103] and believe that persistence and prayer will give us anything we want, including electronic gadgets, a closet full of shoes, and a winning lottery ticket. But two verses later, we learn that Jesus wasn't talking about computers, shoes, or money; he was talking about Spiritual enrichment: *"If you then, who are evil, know how to give good gifts to your children, how much more will the heavenly Father give the Holy Spirit to those who ask him!"*[104]

As I struggle with this topic, it seems to me that Jesus, in his poverty, redefined wealth and now offers us two ways to understand and experience it: **Impoverished Wealth** and **Abundant Wealth** (*my words, not his*). Between these two ideas is the tension he identified as the *problem* of wealth—not how much or how little we have, but how we *feel* about it.

> *No one can serve two masters; for a slave will either hate the one and love the other, or be devoted to the one and despise the other. You cannot serve God and wealth.* (Matthew 6:24, also Luke 16:13)

---

[103]   Luke 11:9
[104]   Luke 11:13

One way to explore Abundant Wealth and Impoverished Wealth begins in the "blessings and woes" from the sermon on the plain in Luke 6:

> (v. 6) *Blessed are you who are poor, for yours* is *the kingdom of God.*

> (v. 24) *But woe to you who are rich, for you* have received *your consolation.*

> (v. 21) *Blessed are you who are hungry now, for you will be filled.*

> (v. 25) *Woe to you who are full now, for you will be hungry.*

We tend to read these "blessings and woes" as something that will happen in the future—in heaven or at the second coming. But notice that Jesus is speaking also in the past tense (*"you have received your consolation"*) and in the present tense (*"yours is the kingdom of God"*). The Kingdom of God that is coming is also the Kingdom that is present whenever and wherever Jesus is present. The master we choose to serve – the world or God's Kingdom – determines how we *feel* about wealth.

Impoverished Wealth comes from the powerful desire and need for material things.

Jesus is very clear about the temporary nature of material wealth and how foolish it is to build a life based on it:

> *Do not store up for yourselves treasures on earth, where moth and rust consume and where thieves*

> *break in and steal. . . . For where your treasure is,*
> *there your heart will be also. (Matthew 6:19, 21)*

The treasures we store up go beyond our basic need for water, food, clothing, and shelter. They can be anything from a collection of salt and pepper shakers to luxury items such as sports cars, vacation homes, closets full of clothes, and many possessions. We also may place a high value on respect, dignity, self-esteem, safety, security, and success. And we may desire (*and even achieve*) great wealth, fame and power.

There is nothing intrinsically wrong with anything on that list. But when we grow attached to them, when we make sacrifices to have them, and when we allow them to define who we are, we also give our hearts to them. And when we give our hearts and lives to anything that becomes more important to us than God, we have chosen to serve that master. When we do all that, we have the "consolation prize" that leaves us empty and always looking for something to fill the space in our lives where God's peace is not. We have chosen the unrest and vulnerability of loving something that can be taken away from us by a fire or a flood or a thief or a cyber attack or a financial meltdown or a health crisis or death. We have chosen Impoverished Wealth.

Abundant Wealth is a very different way of experiencing the world.

It comes "out of the good treasure of the heart,"[105] and is carried in purses that don't wear out.[106] Abundant Wealth flows from the intelligence, imagination, skill, energy, and opportunity that God has given us. Because of that, it is not ours to use only for personal delights and pleasures. It is the wealth that connects us to all creation, and therefore, we use part of what we have received to worship the Creator, to be good stewards of the created world, and to serve our gracious and

---

[105]   Luke 7:45.
[106]   Luke 12:32.

generous God by serving others with grace and generosity. It makes us part of the Kingdom of God that is here now, because Jesus is present[107]

Jesus' parables (*especially the ones that begin, "The Kingdom of God is like . . ."*) offer insights into what Abundant Wealth might be.

> The Kingdom of God is like the King who forgave a debt for one of his salves, only to learn that the man had refused to do the same for another slave.[108] **Abundant Wealth is the ability to give and receive grace and gratitude.**

> The Kingdom of God is like the man who entrusted his slaves with talents while he went on a journey. Some worked to increase what they received; one buried his in the ground.[109] **Abundant Wealth is using our God-given gifts in a way that honors the One who gave them.**

> The Kingdom of God is like the rich man who feasted sumptuously while a poor man named Lazarus, covered in sores, lay at the man's gate. After he died, he looked up from Hades and saw Lazarus in heaven.[110] **Abundant Wealth is sharing with others what you can while you can.**

> The Kingdom of God is like the dinner guest who took the place of honor and heard Jesus say,

---

[107] Luke 17:20–21.
[108] Matthew 18:23–35.
[109] Matthew 25:14–29.
[110] Luke 16:19–25.

"All who exalt themselves will be humbled."[111] **Abundant Wealth is hospitality, kindness, decency, and respect for others.**

The Kingdom of God is like the Pharisee who thanked God that he was better than other people, and the tax collector who asked God for forgiveness and went home justified (*but not the other*).[112] **Abundant Wealth is being humble, and not judging others.**

The Kingdom of God is like the tiny mustard seed that became the greatest of shrubs.[113] **Abundant Wealth is embracing possibilities.**

The Kingdom of God is like the yeast a woman mixed into flour.[114] **Abundant Wealth is joy.**

The Kingdom of God is like a treasure hidden in a field[115] or a pearl of great value.[116] **Abundant Wealth is valuing God's presence more than anything else.**

Ironically, as Jesus went about trying to explain wealth, he didn't always ask everybody to give up everything, as he did with the Rich Man. In the story of Zacchaeus, he simply announces that he is going home with the tax collector who has become wealthy by defrauding

---

[111]   Luke 14:7–14.
[112]   Luke 18:9–14.
[113]   Matthew 13:31–32.
[114]   Matthew 13:33.
[115]   Matthew 13:44.
[116]   Matthew 13:45–46.

his neighbors. Zacchaeus is moved so deeply by Jesus' presence that he offers to give half of all he has to the poor and return four times over any taxes he has collected falsely. Jesus doesn't ask for more. But why did Zacchaeus get by with giving up only half of all he owned and the Rich Man had to sell everything? That doesn't seem fair, at least by our standards.

Jesus seems to be working from a different understanding of wealth. We see this again in the parable of the Prodigal and his brother.[117] A young man asks for—and receives—his inheritance while his father is still alive, then squanders everything on riotous living and is reduced to abject poverty. He returns home, not as a son, but hoping that he might become a servant in his father's house. Instead, his father welcomes him as a son and throws a party to celebrate. Meanwhile, the dutiful brother, who stayed home and worked in the family business, is so bitter and resentful of the joy and celebration for the Prodigal's return that he refuses to go into his father's house. By our standards, the brother's response is understandable (*even appropriate*) because the Prodigal's troubles seem to be self-inflicted wounds that only he should pay for. And, after all, the brother did give up riotous living in order to stay home and work hard.

Since this is a parable, it doesn't take a seminary education to figure out that *our standards* don't apply. The father, who could use "tough love" and send the Prodigal away, chooses instead to forgive his son's mistakes and restore him to the family. The dutiful brother, who still has all his father's material wealth, turns it into Impoverished Wealth by holding so tightly to his bitter resentment that he cannot feel compassion, hospitality, forgiveness, or even respect for his father. The Prodigal, who came back home to repent his sins and ask for nothing except the opportunity to serve, receives Abundant Wealth that is not money, but is the joy of returning to his father's presence.

---

[117] Luke 15:11–32.

When we choose to serve God and embrace the moral and ethical responsibilities we have to one another as children of God, our hearts find a home. When that homecoming also includes a detachment from the desire or need for the riches of the world, we have chosen a Spiritual abundance that fills us up no matter how much—or how little—we own. We don't have to sell everything (*or anything*) because what we have *is not* the master we serve. We have chosen Abundant Wealth.

In Mark's Gospel, the story of the Rich Man offers an important insight that is easy to overlook: *"Jesus, looking at him, loved him."* Asking this man to sell everything and give the money to the poor was not a test or a judgment or a reprimand; it was an act of love. Jesus knew that if the Rich Man continued to want and need his wealth more than he wanted and needed him, the man was doomed to a life of emptiness—a life of Impoverished Wealth. Out of love, Jesus offered him Abundant Wealth with God at the center and a deep Spiritual well to sustain him in a life that would be rich in purpose, meaning, and peace. Jesus asked the man to sell all his possessions because he—the Rich Man—loved them *too* much. And on some level, the man knew this because *"he went away grieving, for he had many possessions."* He knew he had chosen a life that was Spiritually impoverished because he could not give up what he loved more.

The early Christians seemed to understand Abundant Wealth, at least for a while:

> *Awe came upon everyone, because many wonders and signs were being done by the apostles. All who believed were together and had all things in common; they would sell their possessions and goods and distribute the proceeds to all, as any had need. Day by day, as they spent much time together in the temple, they broke bread at home and ate their food with glad and generous hearts, praising God and having the goodwill of all the people. And day by day the Lord added to their number those who were being saved.* (Acts 2:43–47)

Other New Testament writers also spoke to this Christian understanding of wealth:[118]

> *As for those who in the present age are rich, command them not to be haughty, or to set their hopes on the uncertainty of riches, but rather on God who richly provides us with everything for our enjoyment. They are to do good, to be rich in good works, generous, and ready to share, thus storing up for themselves the treasure of a good foundation for the future, so that they may take hold of the life that really is life.* (1 Timothy 6:17–19)

Abundant Wealth does not exalt or excuse poverty.

There have been times in history when Jesus' teachings about wealth and poverty[119] were used to help maintain economic systems in which wealth was concentrated among a few, while many people lived in poverty. Promises of an afterlife that included warm rooms, and streets of gold have sometimes kept those who had little from having *any* aspirations that their lives might be different. Abundant Wealth does not accept poverty as inevitable, but expects that our responses to it will be active and guided by the moral and ethical expectations, born in the Old Testament and embodied in Jesus' life and ministry, that those who have much will help those who have little find fullness in this life. When we are able to do that with, and for, others our lives and the lives around us are enriched.

---

[118] See also James 2:2–8; 1 Peter 4:9–11.

[119] *"Blessed are you who are poor, for yours is the kingdom of God. Blessed are you who are hungry now, for you will be filled. Blessed are you who weep now, for you will laugh. Blessed are you when people hate you, and when they exclude you, revile you, and defame you on account of the Son of Man. Rejoice in that day and leap for joy, for surely your reward is great in heaven."* (Luke 6:20–23).

The world clearly favors Impoverished Wealth.

We live in a world that builds monuments to wealth and promotes the allure of wealth through advertising, easy credit, all-you-can-eat buffets, media fascination with the rich and famous, and a general sense that more of anything is better and new is better than old, until old is old enough to cost more. We may look back longingly to the 1950's America of *Father Knows Best*,[120] but few of us could manage with the modest closet space in those "perfect" homes that housed "perfect" families. Instead, we give fifteen minutes of fame to hoarders, not to people who carry everything they own in a plastic garbage bag. And it all works well until a fire or a flood or a thief or a cyber attack or a financial meltdown or a health crisis or death takes everything away.

This is human nature: putting our trust in our own ingenuity and hard work, our own cleverness and self-interest, looking into the abyss when what we make falls apart, and then reinventing ourselves. It is our cycle of something other than life. Of course, Impoverished Wealth *is* good for the consumer economy, since it keeps us coming back for more—always trying to find the elusive thing that will satisfy some unnamed need.[121] In this climate, the glitz and false promises of Impoverished Wealth inevitably spill over into our political process.

Most of what we debate and vote on eventually comes down to money and possessions: balancing budgets, tax codes, inheritance laws, campaign finance, national security, public education, public safety, unemployment, job training, food stamps, minimum wage, environmental regulations, farm subsidies, energy production, bridges, highways, space programs, scientific research, international agreements

---

120   *Father Knows Best* was a TV series (1954-1960), starring Robert Young and Jane Wyatt.

121   Jesus addressed this in the parable of the sower. The seeds that fell among thorns could not grow because "the cares of the world, and the lure of wealth, and the desire for other things come in and choke the word, and it yields nothing." (Mark 4:19)

and treaties, prison conditions and reform, salaries for elected officials (*you finish the list*). And most government actions eventually result in some redistribution of wealth in some direction—up *and* down the economic ladder.

There is no law that says elected officials (*in their deliberations*) or reporters (*in their commenting*) or citizens (*in their voting*) must consider how Jesus redefined wealth by choosing to live among us in poverty. And yet if we claim to be Christians, we hear Jesus speak to us as the One who is untouched by moths and rust and thieves in the night. We hear him say that being enthralled with riches—either individually or collectively—is a form of Impoverished Wealth that rarely serves us well in the long run. And then we choose the master we serve.

Summary: Coming to live among us in poverty, Jesus changed how we understand wealth from an accounting of how much or how little we own to the way we *feel* about money and what it can or cannot buy. He identified the problem of wealth as the profound tension between trying to serve two masters—wealth or God. In his life and teaching, he shows us two ways of thinking about money and possessions.

Impoverished Wealth is the wealth we believe we have created entirely on our own. Therefore, it belongs to us, and we belong to it. It is the wealth for which we feel a great desire, and need, that is never satisfied. It is the wealth we will do anything to have, even if it means abandoning ethical principles. It is the wealth to which we give our hearts and from which we expect a feeling of completion that never seems to come because of the nagging sense that everything we have is transitory and can be taken away by forces beyond our control. This is the wealth that causes us to be cautious and fearful of anyone who may threaten the world we believe we have created, and to be envious and contemptuous of others who seem to have more. The sense of entitlement we feel from Impoverished Wealth encourages us to use it only to serve our lifestyle and ignore the needs of others—even to the point of exploiting and taking advantage of those who *have* less because we feel they *are* less. Impoverished Wealth is the master we serve that repays us with a great Spiritual emptiness.

Abundant Wealth is the wealth we believe has come from the intelligence, imagination, skill, energy, and opportunity God has given us. Because of that, it is not ours to use only for personal delights and pleasures. It is the wealth that connects us to all of creation, and therefore, we use part of what we have received to worship the Creator, to be good stewards of the created world, and to serve our gracious and generous God by serving others with grace and generosity. Abundant Wealth does not exalt or excuse poverty; instead, it expects us to respond to poverty as Scripture teaches and as Jesus shows us in his life and ministry. The sense of gratitude we feel from having Abundant Wealth moves us toward others and is the wellspring of Christian compassion and charity. Abundant Wealth (*regardless of how few or how many materials things we have*) is not the master we serve; it is the source of Spiritual fullness that gives us peace because we know we have given our hearts to the One who cannot be taken from us.

Wealth and Politics: Much of what we debate and vote on from local city council meetings to the halls of Congress eventually comes down to money and possessions. And many government actions eventually result in some redistribution of wealth in some direction—up and down the economic ladder.

When we claim to be Christians, we should put aside the need to blame, vilify, and shout at each other about the issues of wealth and poverty so we can hear what God in Christ is saying. And what he says most often is the same thing he said to the Rich Man who wanted to know how to have eternal life. Being enthralled with riches—either individually or collectively—is a form of Impoverished Wealth that rarely serves any of us well in the long run. And then we choose the master we serve.

Jesus has the last word:

> *Therefore I tell you, do not worry about your life, what you will eat or what you will drink, or about your body, what you will wear. Is not life more than food, and the body more than clothing?*

> *Look at the birds of the air; they neither sow nor reap nor gather into barns, and yet your heavenly Father feeds them. Are you not of more value than they?*

> *And can any of you by worrying add a single hour to your span of life? And why do you worry about clothing? Consider the lilies of the field, how they grow; they neither toil nor spin, yet I tell you, even Solomon in all his glory was not clothed like one of these.*

> *But if God so clothes the grass of the field, which is alive today and tomorrow is thrown into the oven, will he not much more clothe you—you of little faith? Therefore do not worry, saying, "What will we eat?" or "What will we drink?" or "What will we wear?" For it is the Gentiles who strive for all these things; and indeed your heavenly Father knows that you need all these things.*

> *But strive first for the kingdom of God and his righteousness, and all these things will be given to you as well.* (Matthew 6:25–33)

Chapter 6

God and the Other

What happens when the neighbor Jesus says we must love is also a foreigner, a stranger, even an enemy?

Say the words *immigration, foreigner,* or *alien,* and you will hear strong emotions and language from both sides of the political divide. The issue is as current as the latest tweet and as old as human history. Ironically, in a country built by wave after wave of immigrants and refugees from all around the world, there seems to be a great impulse to pull up the "welcome" mat each time the most recent wave has settled in.

Attitudes about immigration tend to fluctuate with economic conditions and our overall sense of safety and security. For instance, during the building of the transcontinental railroads, we encouraged Asian immigrants, who supplied much of the labor. Then during WWII, Japanese descendants of those workers (*some with children serving in the military*) were taken from the homes and businesses they had built as citizens and were confined in settlements because the collective fear of the enemy had spilled over onto them.

Since reactions to immigration tend to be more visceral than intellectual, the information that feeds those reactions comes from stories and antidotes more often than from statistics and facts. And since stories about dangerous and threatening behavior (*or heart-rending scenes of parents and children in desperate situations*) very often increase media ratings, those become the visual and emotional images that influence how we think and feel about foreigners, either with suspicion or with sympathy.

Campaign rallies, speeches from the halls of Congress, television interviews, debates around the water cooler at work, conversations over meals with family and friends, and tweets and comments over social media from everywhere amplify the emotional noise even more. At issue is the complex legal system around immigration: how it may or may not (*should or should not*) be changed and why. How we approach this issue often depends on cultural norms, tribal instincts, historical experiences, and gut feelings.

Those of us who are Christians also may want to know what the Bible says. And on this matter, there seems to be something for everyone:

If you want to build walls, overhaul financial institutions, reduce taxes, and achieve cultural purity by deporting foreigners, look to the books of Ezra and Nehemiah.

The story begins in 539 BCE, when King Cyrus of Persia (*modern-day Iran*) defeated Babylon and ordered the Jews who had been exiles in Babylon to return to Judah, where they would start rebuilding the Temple in Jerusalem. In 458 BCE, Ezra, a priest and scribe, arrived with another wave of exiles to create a "true Israel." Ezra appointed magistrates, enacted worship reforms, and transferred property *from* those who had remained and worked in Judah *to* the returning exiles. He also purified the culture by ending marriages with foreigners,[122] and leading the country in a public divorce and deportation of all foreign wives and their children.[123]

Thirteen years later, Nehemiah came from Babylon with Persian authority and more exiles to rebuild the wall around Jerusalem, fortify the city, and oversee its repopulation. Unfortunately, his building project also worsened a financial crisis in the making from the perfect storm of Persian taxes on land and crops, a drought that reduced farm production, a labor shortage during the harvest because all men were required to work (*without pay*) on the wall, and high interest rates on loans by Jewish creditors that caused borrowers to pledge fields,

---

[122]   *"After these things had been done, the officials approached me and said, 'The people of Israel, the priests, and the Levites have not separated themselves from the people of the lands with their abominations, from the Canaanites, the Hittites, the Perizzites, the Jebusites, the Ammonites, the Moabites, the Egyptians, and the Amorites. For they have taken some of their daughters as wives for themselves and for their sons'"* (Ezra 9:1–2a).

[123]   See Ezra chapters 9–10 for the whole story.

vineyards, houses, and the labor of their sons and daughters as collateral. As creditors started to amass wealth by foreclosing on loans, the people came to Nehemiah with their complaints;[124] and he ordered creditors to return the land and the interest they had collected to debtors, while he reformed credit and tax policies. Nehemiah joined Ezra in condemning mixed marriages and led the Jews in efforts to separate themselves from neighboring people—their wives, their sons, and their daughters.[125]

If you are in favor of welcoming immigrants and incorporating them into the fabric of the country, read on:[126]

> *When an alien resides with you in your land, you shall not oppress the alien. The alien who resides with you shall be to you as the citizen among you; you shall love the alien as yourself, for you were aliens in the land of Egypt: I am the LORD your God.* (Leviticus 19:33)

The question of the Other is complex and nuanced in Scripture.

For instance, there are different classifications that don't always mean the same as they do to us today:

Alien (*or sojourner*) was someone who lived in a community that was not his or her family or tribe. In the ancient world, survival depended on the protection and provision of being within a cohesive group. And yet people often found themselves forced to leave their

---

[124] Nehemiah 5:1–5.
[125] Nehemiah 9.
[126] See also Leviticus 19:10; 23:22; 24:22; Numbers 9:14; 15:14-16, 29-30; Deuteronomy 1:16-17; 24:17-21; 27:19; Jeremiah 7:5-7; 22:3-4; Zechariah 7:9-10.

homes because of famine,[127] war, political upheaval, family feuds;[128] to escape punishment;[129] and sometimes because God called them to go elsewhere—Abraham and Sarah, for instance.[130] Therefore, the concepts of community and hospitality became essential—a matter of life and death. Members of communities provided protection and support for each other and extended hospitality to strangers because they knew they could be the next group to need it from others.

Because the Hebrews had been rescued from danger and poverty by the hospitality of others,[131] the Hebrew God commanded that they offer hospitality to the poor and the aliens who came to live among them. Resident aliens lived under the same laws and assumed the same responsibilities as citizens. They could buy and sell property, participate in worship (*circumcision was required to celebrate the Passover*), take part in the assembly, and have access to Cities of Refuge.[132]

Foreigner (*or stranger*) is a term with several different meanings:

First: Non-Israelite travelers who were passing through, traders conducting business (*under special laws of finance and trade*), and soldiers

---

[127]   See Genesis 12:10–20; 26:1–14; 42:5; 45:25; Ruth 1:1.

[128]   See Genesis 27:41–45.

[129]   See Exodus 2:11–15.

[130]   See Genesis 12:1–10.

[131]   Abraham and Sarah in Egypt (Genesis 12:10, 13:2) and in Gerar (Genesis 20:1–17); Isaac's family displaced by a drought (Genesis 26:1–23); Jacob escaping Esau's anger (Genesis 28:1–7); Jacob's family displaced by famine into Egypt (Genesis 37:1, 47:12); Moses seeking refuge in Midian (Exodus 2:11–22); directions for the Passover meal with instructions for including aliens (Exodus 12:48; 13:2); Ruth's in-laws who escaped famine in Bethlehem by moving to Moab (Ruth 1:1).

[132]   See also Exodus 22:21; 23:9-12; Leviticus 16:29; 18:26; 19:10; 23:22; 24:23-24; Numbers 9:14; 15:14-16, 29-30; 35:15; Deuteronomy 1:16; 5:14; 10:17-19; 14:28-29; 24:14-22; 26:4-5; 27:19; Joshua 8:33; Psalm 94:6; 105:23; Jeremiah 7:6-7; 22:3; Zechariah 7:10.

on the way to someplace else. In a world without even a Motel 6, these travelers depended on the hospitality and protection of people in the towns and cities along their journey.[133]

Second: Slaves and non-Israelite freedmen who were not allowed to participate in worship (*even their animals could not be used as sacrifices*). They, too, operated under separate legal and financial systems.[134]

Third: Foreign gods that were always a temptation for the people of Israel.[135]

Fourth: Enemies that threatened and invaded Israel (*sometimes used by God to punish God's people*).[136]

The Bible also points to a future where people will come together:

> *Now the LORD said to Abram, "I will make of you a great nation, and I will bless you, and make your name great, so that . . . in you all the families of the earth shall be blessed."* (Genesis 12:1–3)

---

[133] The worst cases when hospitality was refused include Lot's threatened attack in Sodom (Genesis 19) and the death of the Levite's concubine (Judges 19).

[134] See Genesis 17:12, 27; Exodus 12:43; Nehemiah 9:2; 13:30; Proverbs 20:16; 27:13; Ezekiel 31:12; 44:7–9; Leviticus 22:25.

[135] See Genesis 35:2; Deuteronomy 31:16; 32:12-16; Joshua 24:20-23; Judges 10:16; 1 Samuel 7:3; 2 Chronicles 14:3; 33:15; Psalm 81:9-10; 44:20-21; Isaiah 17:10-14; 43:11-13; Jeremiah 2:25; 3:13; 5:10-13; 8:19.

[136] See 2 Samuel 22:45–46; Psalm 18:44–45; 109:11; 144:7; Isaiah 1:7; 2:6; 25:2–5; 62:8; Ezekiel 7:21; 11:9;, 28:7–10;, 30:12;, 31:12; Hosea 7:9;, 8:7; Obadiah 1:11.

And the foreigners who join themselves to the
LORD . . . I will bring to my holy mountain, and
make them joyful in my house of prayer . . . for
my house shall be called a house of prayer for all
peoples. (Isaiah 56:6–7)

The birth of Jesus Christ turned everything upside down.

Hidden in Matthew's "Genealogy of Jesus the Messiah" (*which
almost nobody ever reads because of all the hard-to-pronounce names*)
is an interesting counterbalance to the complaints Ezra heard about
the foreigners who had defiled Judah (*Canaanites, Hittites, Perizzites,
Jebusites, Ammonites, Moabites, Egyptians, and Amorites*).[137] Matthew's
list of ancestors that starts with Abraham and moves forward to Mary's
husband, Joseph, begins in chapter 1 and includes the following:

> (v. 3) ***Judah the father of Perez and Zerah
> by Tamar*** (Tamar was the Canaanite widow of
> Judah's oldest son. She tricked Judah into giving
> her children: Perez, whose descendants were the
> Perezzites; and Zerah, whose descendants were
> the Zerahites.)[138]

> (v. 5a) ***Salmon the father of Boaz by Rahab***
> (Rahab probably was the Canaanite prostitute
> who, at her peril, hid the spies Joshua sent to
> Jericho in advance of the battle to take the
> Promised Land. Because of her courage and
> faithfulness, Rahab and her entire family
> were spared and became part of the Israelite
> community.)[139]

---

[137]   Ezra 9:1–2a.
[138]   See Genesis 38:6–24; Numbers 26:20.
[139]   See Joshua 2:1; 6:25; Hebrews 11:31; James 2:25.

(v. 5b–6a) ***Boaz the father of Obed by Ruth,
and Obed the father of Jesse, and Jesse the
father of King David*** (Ruth was the widowed
Moabite who followed her mother-in-law to
Bethlehem where Ruth was able to provide
food for them in their poverty by gleaning at
the edges of fields owned by Boaz. He noticed
her, married her, and she became the great-
grandmother of King David.)[140]

(v. 6b) ***David was the father of Solomon by
the wife of Uriah.*** (The wife of Uriah was
Bathsheba, whom David saw bathing on her
rooftop [*where people bathed*] because he lived
in the house that looked down on all the other
houses and because he had not left the city to
lead his army [*as the king was expected to do*]. He
sent for her, she became "with child," and David
had Uriah killed in battle so he could marry her.
Bathsheba would have been considered a Hittite
by Jewish law because she married Uriah.)[141]

Matthew's genealogy has different names than those found in
Luke's genealogy[142] (*that begins with Joseph and traces back to Adam*)
because neither was writing about biology, even though both, ironically,
provide family trees that point to Joseph as Jesus' father. Each of them
was making a theological statement. Luke (*who was likely a Gentile*)
establishes Jesus as the Son of God in the context of Jewish history.
Matthew (*who was a Jew*) suggests that the coming of the Messiah is
for all people—men and women, saints and sinners, rich and poor,
powerful and powerless, Jews and Gentiles, even the wise men from the

---

[140]   See the book of Ruth.
[141]   See 2 Samuel 11:3; 12:24; Psalm 51.
[142]   See Matthew 1:1–17; Luke 3:23–38.

east who showed up at the manger. Both are right. And in his life and ministry, Jesus establishes the truth of both claims.

He will be called Son of God.[143]

This announcement, given by an angel in the days of King Herod of Judea to a young woman named Mary, establishes the intersection of earthly time and place with the great mystery of God taking on flesh and coming to live among us as a man who was born to a Jewish woman in a Jewish family, a Jewish community, and a Jewish religion.

As an infant, he was circumcised and dedicated to the Lord in the Temple,[144] and he and his family retraced the path of God's people to Egypt and back to Judah.[145]

As a boy, he went every year with his parents to celebrate the Passover in Jerusalem and amazed everyone who heard and observed him in serious discussions with the rabbis.[146]

As a man, Jesus of Nazareth was baptized in the Jordan River, where a voice from heaven announced, "You are my Son, the Beloved."[147] He demonstrated Divine power and authority by casting out demons, forgiving sins, healing people, and performing miracles.[148] He visited the Temple and taught in synagogues, where he read from

---

[143]   See Luke 1:35.
[144]   Luke 2:22–38.
[145]   Matthew 2:13–23.
[146]   Luke 2:41–52.
[147]   See Matthew 3:13–17; Mark 1:9–11; Luke 3:21; John 1:29–34.
[148]   See Matthew 8:5-13; 8:28-9:8; 9:18-26; 12:9-21; 14:13-21; 14:34-36; 15:21-31; 17:14-21; 20:29-34; Mark 1:21-28; 2:1-12; 3:1-12; 5:1-43; 6:30-56; 7:31-37; 9:14-29; 10:46-52; Luke 4:31-40; 5:12-26; 6:6-11; 7:1-17; 8:26-56; 9:10-17, 37-43; 11:14-23; 13:10-17; 14:1-6; 17:11-19; 18:35-43; John 2:1-12; 4:46-5:18; 6:1-14, 16-21; 8:1-11; 9:1-41; 11:1-44.

sacred texts.[149] Jesus' followers only gradually came to understand his unique distinction when they saw him walking on water and ordering powerful winds to be still;[150] and at the Transfiguration as he stood with Moses, who represented the Law, and Elijah, who represented the prophets, while God's voice once again announced, "This is my Son, the Beloved."[151] Even then, despite Peter's declaration that Jesus was the Messiah,[152] they were not quite sure what it all meant—for them and for the world.[153] "Son of God" was part of the accusations and taunts at his trial and crucifixion.[154] Perhaps the most memorable self-revelation of his identity is in these words that are familiar to most, if not all, Christians:

> *For God so loved the world that he gave his only Son, so that everyone who believes in him may not perish but may have eternal life. Indeed, God did not send the Son into the world to condemn the world, but in order that the world might be saved through him.* (John 3:16–17)

Jesus will become a foreigner and stranger among his people in order to welcome foreigners and strangers into God's Kingdom.

As the fulfillment of God's intention to "bless all the nations" and build a "house of prayer for all people," Jesus traveled outside prescribed boundaries and borders that separated people culturally, theologically, politically, and geographically. And he drew them together.

---

149   See Matthew 4:23-25; 12:9-13; 13:54; Mark 1:21-29, 35-39; 3:1-6; 6:1-6; Luke 4:16-30, 33-38, 42-44; 6:6-11; 59-61.
150   See Matthew 14:22–33; Mark 6:45–52; John 6:15–21.
151   See Matthew 17:1–13; Mark 9:2–13; Luke 9:28–36; 2 Peter 1:16–18.
152   See Matthew 16:13–20; Mark 8:27–30; Luke 9:18–20.
153   See John 1:1; 29–34; 45–51; 5:24–29; 20:30–31.
154   See Matthew 26:59–63; 27:40; Luke 22:70; 23:1; John 19:6–7.

At the most fundamental level, he was rejected as a prophet in his hometown,[155] and he rejected the traditional idea of his or any family unit:

> *Whoever loves father or mother more than me is not worthy of me; and whoever loves son or daughter more than me is not worthy of me.* (Matthew 10:37)[156]

He also defined his new family:

> *My mother and my brothers are those who hear the word of God and do it.* (Luke 8:21)[157]

Jesus challenged cultural and religious customs when he touched a leper in order to heal him and, again, when he intervened to stop the stoning of a woman caught in adultery.[158] During dinner at the home of a Pharisee, he allowed a woman of the streets (*a sinner*) to anoint his feet with expensive oil and then he forgave her. When the Pharisee complained, Jesus pointed out that the host had neglected the most basic gesture of hospitality—providing water to wash his feet.[159]

He crossed political boundaries when he healed the servant of a Roman Centurion,[160] when he included a tax collector among his disciples and dined with Zacchaeus,[161] when he condemned cities that had not accepted his ministry,[162] and when he spoke of the Kingdom

---

[155]   See Matthew 13:54-58; Mark 6:1-6; Luke 4:16-30.
[156]   See Luke 12:51–53; 14:26–27.
[157]   See Matthew 12:46–50; Mark 3:31–35.
[158]   See Matthew 8:1–4; Mark 1:40–45; Luke 5:12–16; John 8:1–11.
[159]   Luke 7:36–50.
[160]   See Matthew 8:5-13; Luke 7:1-10.
[161]   See Matthew 10:3; Luke 5:27; 19:2–10.
[162]   See Matthew 11:20–24; Luke 10:13–15.

of God as if it were the New Promised Land—the new homeland for God's new people.[163]

He crossed geographic borders that separated Judah from Gentile territory. In the country of the Gerasenes,[164] he healed the ultimate Other—a Gentile who was homeless and naked, living in a perpetual state of ritual uncleanness in the tombs, possessed by so many demons his condition would have been considered a sign of severe evil. When Jesus asked his name, his reply was heartbreaking because he had none but called himself "Legion." Jesus restored him to wholeness and broke the Torah to make it happen.

In the region of Tyre and Sidon,[165] a Syrophoenician woman (*Canaanite in Matthew's Gospel*) begs him to heal her daughter. The disciples urge him to send her away, and even he says, "It is not fair to take the children's food and throw it to the dogs." But Jesus is so moved by this kneeling, pleading woman he is convinced, and her daughter is healed instantly. From there, a crowd followed him to a mountain where he cured the lame, the maimed, the blind, the mute, and many others, then he fed four thousand people[166] (*just as they had fed five thousand in Bethsaida*).

Who is my neighbor? Who is my enemy?

When a lawyer asked Jesus about inheriting eternal life, the lawyer recited the answer attributed to Jesus in Matthew and Mark:

> *You shall love the Lord your God with all your*
> *heart, and with all your soul, and with all your*

---

[163]   See Matthew 8:10–11; 12:27–28; 21:31; 21:42–45; Mark 1:14–15; 9:1; 10:14–15; 12:28–34; Luke 4:42–43; 8:1, 9:1–2; 9:11; 10:8–11; 17:20–21; John 3:3–5.

[164]   See Matthew 8:29–9:1; Mark 5:1-20; Luke 8:26-39.

[165]   See Matthew 15:21–28; Mark 7:24–30.

[166]   See Matthew 15:29–39; Mark 7:31–37; 8:1–10.

strength, and with all your mind; and your neighbor as yourself. (Luke 10: 27)

Then the man asked, "Who is my neighbor?"

Jesus responded with the parable of the Good Samaritan,[167] forcing the lawyer to admit that the neighbor in the story was not the priest or the Levite who has passed by a beaten traveler without offering help. The neighbor was "the one who showed mercy."[168] Trouble is, "the one who showed mercy" was a Samaritan, and Samaritans and Jews had been enemies for over seven hundred years. What happens when the neighbor we are commanded to love is also the enemy?

Well, if you are Jesus, you go to him or, in this case, her. Although one Samaritan village refused to receive him,[169] we read about another village where he encounters a woman at Jacob's well.[170] Over the years, so much attention has been given to this woman's marital history[171] that it is possible to miss an important point: Jesus doesn't

---

[167] See Matthew 22:34-40; Mark 12:28-34; Luke 10:25-37.

[168] Instead of saying "The Good Samaritan," the lawyer can only bring himself to say, "The one who showed mercy," indicating how deep the divide was between Samaritans and Jews. This history of enmity between these two populations (based on ethnic, cultural, and religious differences) is essential to understanding how radical it was for Jesus to tell this story as an answer to the lawyer's question: "Who is my neighbor?"

[169] Luke 9:51–56.

[170] John 4:1–42.

[171] The woman at the well may have had five husbands because of immoral behavior. Or it may have resulted from the custom of Levirate marriage, where the next younger brother would marry his brother's widow. And in a land where people often died young, it would not be unusual for her to have been widowed more than once and married five brothers in succession. We don't know. We do know that she was alone, excluded by the women of the city from their circle. In those days, gathering water was something women did together early in the morning before breakfast and in the cool of the evening. And yet this woman came in the heat of the day when nobody else was at the well.

seem to care about her past and mentions it only to reveal something about who *he* is, not to judge her. He doesn't tell her to "go and sin no more," as he does with others. In fact, the word *sin* is never used in this story. (*That's something we have read into the text.*)

She knows immediately that he is a Jew who is breaking Jewish law even by speaking to her and drinking from her jug, and she asks the question that separates her people from his: "Who is right about where to worship God—Jews or Samaritans?" He answers, "True worshippers will worship the Father in Spirit and in truth. The place doesn't matter. The time has come for these divisions to be over." She is the first person in John's Gospel to have a theological discussion with Jesus. In fact, he talks with her longer than he talks with anyone else in all four Gospels; and because of her witness, many will come to faith.

As Jesus traveled toward Jerusalem for the last time, he told his disciples another story that started, "*For the kingdom of heaven is like . . .*" This time it is like hiring laborers in a vineyard,[172] where those who are hired at the end of the day are paid the same as those who have been working since morning. He was saying that there no longer would be pride of place for those who have been God's people through long tradition. They must make room to include foreigners, strangers, even old enemies in the Kingdom that is here now because he is present.

And that's exactly what happened after the resurrection and Pentecost, when Jesus' followers accepted his final commission[173] to "go into all the world," and the new church (*his church*) exploded with foreigners and strangers from the Middle East, Europe, and Africa with different cultures, languages, races, and philosophies, including the household of Cornelius the Centurion (*of the Italian cohort*)[174] converted

---

[172] Matthew 20:1–16.
[173] See Matthew 28:16-20; Mark 16:14-18; Luke 24:36-39; John 20:19-23; Acts 1:6-8.
[174] Acts 10:1–35.

by Peter, the household of Lydia[175] (*in modern-day Turkey*) converted by Paul, and the Ethiopia eunuch (*African*) baptized by Philip.[176] The apostle Paul, who provided the spark for expansion, declared (*in the first Bible verse I was asked to memorize by a Sunday school teacher*),

> For there is no difference between the Jew and the Greek; for the same Lord over all is rich unto all that call upon him. (Romans 10:12, KJV)

What does this say to us about the Other?

What started as a discussion about immigration has been expanded by what Scripture says about the life and ministry of Jesus Christ. Yes, the Other includes foreigners and strangers from different countries and regions, *and* it includes those among us (*regardless of citizenship*) who are "different"—separate from the mainstream because of race, religion, gender, occupation, financial status, education, physical appearance, mental condition, and anything else that feeds our very human inclination toward prejudice and protection for what feels normal to us. What we choose to do politically about the complex issues of immigration and the Other probably will continue to be influenced in the same ways those choices always have been—by economic forces and our sense of safety and well-being.

As Christians, we have a legacy that includes occasions when God's people separated themselves from their neighbors (*and even annihilated men, women, children, and animals*)[177] in order to preserve cultural and religious purity. *And* we have Jesus Christ, who (*beginning with his genealogy and birth*) brought a new understanding that says

---

175   Acts 16:14–15.
176   Acts 8:27–38.
177   See Joshua 6:17–21; 7:1–15; Judges 1:17.

foreigners, strangers, outcasts, and the "different" are the neighbors we must love, even when they are enemies.

We live within the tension of both worldviews and struggle with the difficult discipleship Jesus asks of us—a discipleship that even he admits is impossible on our own.[178] What we can do, at the very least, is remember that Christianity doesn't belong to us. It belongs to Christ, and we are part of the Body of Christ because we have been invited, along with others who may be foreigners and strangers to us but not to him.[179] We can remember that Jesus reserved his most scathing judgment for those who used positions of power to exclude and marginalize the very people some of us would like to exclude and marginalize today.[180] We can remember that he didn't just accept the Other. He walked miles to find them, and he changed their lives through his compassion, not power.

Even when we find it difficult to love the inconvenient and hard-to-love neighbors Jesus gives us, we (*all of us: candidates, elected officials, reporters, commentators, and voters*) can honor him by speaking about them with words that are respectful and worthy of the sacrifice he made for us. We can acknowledge that we worship a God who is love and avoid doing or saying anything that looks like or sounds like hatred. We can try.

Summary: *Immigration, foreigner,* and *alien* have become incendiary words that cause strong emotions and language on both sides of

---

[178] *When the disciples heard this, they were greatly astounded and said, "Then who can be saved?" But Jesus looked at them and said, "For mortals it is impossible, but for God all things are possible."* (Matthew 19:25–26)

[179] *Beloved, you do faithfully whatever you do for the friends, even though they are strangers to you. . . . Therefore we ought to support such people, so that we may become co-workers with them.* (3 John 5a, 8)

[180] See Matthew 9:11; 19:3; 22:15–19; 23:13–36; Mark 2:16–17; Luke 5:17–32.

the political divide. At issue is the complex legal system around immigration. Our responses to the question of what to do about the Other have become more visceral than intellectual—driven by stories about dangerous and threatening behavior or heart-rending scenes of parents and children in desperate situations. Campaign rallies, speeches from the halls of Congress, television interviews, debates around the water cooler at work, conversations over meals with family and friends, and tweets and comments over social media from everywhere amplify the emotional noise even more. How we approach this issue often depends on cultural norms, tribal instincts, personal experiences, and gut feelings.

Christians who look to the Bible for guidance can find occasions when God's people separated themselves from their neighbors in order to preserve cultural and religious purity. *And* there are commandments that require us to provide hospitality for strangers and treat the alien as a citizen.[181] The coming of Jesus Christ clarified, and expanded, these different understandings of the Other.

Matthew's genealogy of Jesus mentions women who represent multicultural inclusion in the mystery of God Incarnate. In his life and ministry, Jesus became a stranger among his own people and his religion in order to bring foreigners and strangers into the all-inclusive Kingdom that God intended and Jesus proclaimed. He challenged cultural and religious customs, crossed political boundaries and geographic borders, and in a theological discussion with a Samaritan woman by a well, he established that the time for division among people was over. When a young lawyer asked, "Who is my neighbor?" he responded with the parable of the Good Samaritan and introduced the radical idea that the neighbors we are commanded to love might also include our enemies.

Jesus reached out to those who were excluded from belonging anywhere because they were "not our kind of people"—separate from

---

[181]   See Leviticus 19:9–10; 19:33; Deuteronomy 24:17–18.

the mainstream because of race, religion, gender, occupation, financial status, education, physical appearance, and mental condition. He made them his kind of people and said, "If you're with me, you have to understand that these folks are coming too. And if you want me for a friend, you have to find a way to become friends with them just as I did."

After the resurrection and Pentecost, the new Christian community exploded with foreigners and strangers from the Middle East, Europe, and Africa with different cultures, languages, races, and philosophies. The apostle Paul, who provided the spark for expansion, declared,

> *For there is no difference between the Jew and the Greek; for the same Lord over all is rich unto all that call upon him.* (Romans 10:12, KJV)

How we respond to this inconvenient Jesus who brings us hard-to-love neighbors is a challenge. At the very least, we can honor him by speaking about them with words that are respectful and worthy of the sacrifice he made for all of us. We can remind ourselves that Christianity doesn't belong to us. It belongs to Christ, and we are part of the Body of Christ because we have been invited, along with others who may be foreigners and strangers to us but not to him. We can acknowledge that we worship a God who is love and avoid doing or saying anything that looks like, or sounds like, hatred. We can try.

Jesus has the last word:

> *Woman, believe me, the hour is coming when you will worship the Father neither on this mountain nor in Jerusalem. But the hour is coming, and is now here, when the true worshipers will worship the Father in spirit and truth, for the Father seeks such as these to worship him.* (John 4:21, 23)

Chapter 7

God and Political Power

Relitigating the infinite possibilities of
"who has the right to make who do (or not do) what"
does little to show anyone the character and
purpose of God revealed in Jesus Christ.

There must be a better way.

Scripture was written long before our modern understanding of democracy. So trying to figure out what the Bible says about political power, as we experience it, takes some digging into the past.

In the beginning, God expected creation to follow Divine instruction in the choices they made and how they would live together. Then after the first two chapters in the book of Genesis, deception, mayhem, and murder ruined the plan.[182] Still, we find remarkable occasions when God spoke, and people did what God asked: Noah built an Ark.[183] Abraham and Sarah left everything they knew and went to "a place I will show you."[184] Abraham trusted the Lord so much he even was willing to sacrifice Isaac (*the son finally born when he and Sarah were in their nineties*).[185] Moses reluctantly answered the call from a burning bush and convinced Pharaoh to release the Hebrews who had become slaves in Egypt.[186]

In the wilderness, God used Moses to shape a loosely organized confederation of tribes into "this people"[187] who could take and occupy the Promised Land.[188] "This people" received the beginning of a social structure and an understanding of the responsibilities of leadership through the Torah[189]—the Law that provides instruction and a moral framework for living together as God's people. Although the Ten Commandments are part of the Torah, it covers many functions of being together in community:[190]

---

[182]   Genesis 3:4 – 4:25.

[183]   Genesis 6:11 – 9:28.

[184]   Genesis 12:1-9.

[185]   Genesis 22:1-19

[186]   Exodus 3:1-12.

[187]   God and Moses consistently use "this people," not "these people" that would indicate a group of individuals. "This people" referred to the *kahal,* the congregation, the mutually dependent community.

[188]   Exodus 13:17 – 19:25.

[189]   In Hebrew, *Torah* means "instruction."

[190]   For more details about God's instructions, see Exodus 20:1 through Leviticus 27:34.

Justice—that requires caring for the poor, the oppressed, the lame, the refugee, and the alien

Hygiene and cleanliness—that covers disease, death, burial, bodily discharge, hand washing, and other matters

Social customs—related to marriage, divorce, food preparation, land ownership, commerce, fairness to workers, inheritance, and more

Worship and holiness—offerings, atonement, general behavior, obedience, festivals, and Jubilee

They also were given the foundation for a legal code that would continue to expand:[191]

You shall not spread a false report. You shall not join hands with the wicked to act as a malicious witness.

You shall not follow a majority in wrongdoing; when you bear witness in a lawsuit, you shall not side with the majority so as to pervert justice; nor shall you be partial to the poor in a lawsuit.

You shall not pervert the justice due to your poor in their lawsuits.

In the wilderness, God affirmed that even a charismatic leader cannot effectively manage large groups, and instructed Moses (*who had*

---

[191]   Exodus 23:1-9.

complained, "I am not able to carry all this people alone . . .")[192] to gather seventy of the elders with leadership ability. Some of the Spirit that was on Moses was given to these elders who shared in the responsibilities of governance[193] and who later organized behind Joshua to take the Promised Land.[194]

After Joshua, a series of military leaders called judges[195] ruled the religious and civic life of Israel as it slid into complete depravity. The book of Judges begins with stories of courage, faith, and military victories before unraveling into idolatry, political intrigue, greed, exploitation, rape, murder, and an unholy civil war—all explained by a recurring statement: "In those days, there was no king in Israel; all the people did what was right in their own eyes."[196]

Give us a king so we can be like all the nations.

Ignoring the irony that God was the sovereign they no longer recognized or followed, Israel went to their prophet Samuel and asked him to appoint a "king to govern us" so they could be like everyone else. Samuel knew that a king would usurp his power as their prophet, and he complained to God, "They have rejected me!"

"Rejected you!" God replied. "They've rejected me. It's what they do. What they've always done. Now you know how it feels. But listen to the people. Make sure they know what it is they are asking. And give them what they want."

The people listened as Samuel told them their sons would be taken as soldiers, their daughters would be servants in the elegant

192 Numbers 11:14.
193 Numbers 11:16-17.
194 Deuteronomy 31:23; Joshua 1:1–7.
195 In Hebrew, the word *sopate* (judge) also means "ruler."
196 Judges 17:6; 21:25.

lifestyle of a new aristocracy, they would pay taxes, and would no longer work for themselves but for their king. In spite of his warnings, they said, "Let our king rule over us and go out before us and fight our battles."[197]

In Deuteronomy 17, Moses had told the people about the dangers of having a king. But if they felt they must, their king should follow these rules: [198] He should read the Torah "all the days of his life." He should not exalt himself among the people or acquire great wealth. He should not have many wives. Most of all, he should not keep horses. To put "keeping horses" in modern terms, horses (*especially horses and chariots*) were the standing army in those days. They represented the human institutions that Israel would create and depend on for their protection and well-being, instead of trusting and relying on God.

Well, they got their king but lost the Torah. Workers found the "Book of God's Law"[199] four hundred years later when King Josiah was renovating the Temple. Meanwhile, most of the kings became obscenely wealthy; they had many wives (*sometimes foreign wives, sometimes the wives of other men*),[200] they worshiped foreign gods, and they kept horses—lots of horses.[201] Something else happened. The kings established a judicial system that reported to them,[202] and they transformed worship into a

---

[197]   See 1 Samuel 8:5 through 10:8 for the entire story of how Israel got their king.

[198]   Deuteronomy 17:14–20.

[199]   See 2 Kings 22:1–30; 2 Chronicles 34:29–36:1. The "Book of God's Law" might have been Deuteronomy or the entire Pentateuch. Based on this discovery, Josiah destroyed pagan shrines, initiated social reforms, and restored the celebration the Passover (*that had been abandoned after the reign of Solomon*).

[200]   Bathsheba, the wife of Uriah the Hittite, see 2 Samuel 11:1–12:23.

[201]   1 Kings 11:1–6 report that Solomon had one thousand wives—many of them foreign—and he worshiped the foreign gods Astarte and Milcom. He also imported many horses. Many of the kings that followed Solomon also ignored the requirements God had given in Deuteronomy 17.

[202]   See 2 Chronicles 22:3-4, 25:16; Isaiah 1:21-31.

state religion, with a Temple[203] to keep their domesticated God in the proper place and priests who were willing to serve political interests.[204] Israel created a kingdom with a wealthy few controlling the many who lived in poverty,[205] where religion supported and even participated in corruption,[206] and where those in power exploited the most vulnerable among them.[207] In their pride and arrogance, they came to believe that the kingdom they had created was also God's kingdom.

You see, when they lost the Torah, they lost the sense of the Holy within them and around them.[208] They lost the obligation to share with the poor and the marginalized, to give hospitality to the alien, to accommodate those with physical disabilities, to care for creation, and to love the neighbor.

When they lost the Torah, they lost the Divine imperative against lying, cheating, and taking what belongs to others; against fraudulent business practices and exploitation of those who labor; against bearing a grudge and getting even; against "hating in your heart." They lost the sovereignty of God over their lives and, instead, came to worship their own cleverness and to hallow (*in the name of God*) their own material and political best interest. In time, the unholy alliance between religion and monarchy contributed to the decline of both northern and southern kingdoms as they unraveled in self-indulgence and corruption and came under the domination of one superpower after another—Assyria, Babylon, Persia, and then in 63 BCE, Rome.

---

203   See 1 Kings 8:1–13; 2 Chronicles 5:7–6:1.

204   See 2 Samuel 15:34-36; 1 Kings 12:31-33; 13:33; 2 Kings 17:1-41; 2 Chronicles 11:13-15; 12:1-9.

205   See Amos, especially 3:15–4:1; Micah 1:1–2:11.

206   Micah 3:11.

207   Micah 7:3.

208   See Leviticus 19:1–37 and Deuteronomy 15:1–23 for information about what the Torah says concerning moral and ethical requirements listed in these two paragraphs.

Rome used political and religious power to maintain *pax romana*.

In order to avoid civil unrest and maintain Roman peace (*pax romana)*, the occupying forces in first-century Palestine appropriated political and religious institutions already in place: the Sanhedrin (*the Jewish council*), the Herodian kings, and the religious leaders (*Sadducees, Pharisees, priests, and scribes*). Rome used these institutions to keep the people under control and allowed them only the power necessary to serve Rome's interests. They, in turn, used the Roman officials and military as instruments to achieve their own ends when they could.[209] Meanwhile, the people longed for the Day of the Lord—when God's chosen one, the Messiah, would come with an army to intervene in history and establish a better earthly kingdom of peace and prosperity—for them, of course.

In the fullness of time, the promised Messiah did come—Jesus of Nazareth—to fulfill all the hope of Israel and establish the Kingdom of God among human beings. But he was not the great warrior they expected. He was the son of a carpenter who became an itinerate preacher, with no home and with a rag-tag group of followers who traveled with him. If life on the road weren't difficult enough, his teaching and ministry took place in an ongoing, high-stakes theological dispute with religious leaders.

- He reframed the Law concerning everything from anger and adultery to enemies and prayer with *"You have heard it said . . . but, I tell you . . ."*[210]

---

[209] The trial and crucifixion of Jesus of Nazareth, carried out by Rome, was requested by Jewish leaders because they could not take that action on their own. They were able to convince Roman authorities that the throngs of people who were gathering around Jesus could erupt in a rebellion. And so it was done.

[210] See Matthew 5:21-7:5; 19:9; Luke 6:27-42; 11:2-4, 34-36; 12:22-34, 57-59.

- They criticized him for eating with tax collectors and sinners.[211]

- He used them as examples of hypocritical and unfaithful behavior.[212]

- They tried to trap him with questions about paying taxes to the emperor.[213]

- He broke the Sabbath to heal the sick and pluck grain for food.[214]

- They complained that he and his disciples didn't fast or wash their hands.[215]

- He trapped them with a question about the son of David.[216]

- They challenged his authority, accused him of blasphemy, and declared that he was in league with the devil.[217]

- He denounced them (*"Woe to you . . ."*),[218] and they set in motion the inevitability of his trial and crucifixion.

Against the backdrop of escalating tension with religious and political leaders in general, not all of them opposed him. Jesus dined with the leader of the Pharisees, he met with Nicodemus (*a Pharisee*) in secret to discuss being born again "from above," and after his death, he

---

[211]   See Matthew 9:9–13; Mark 2:13–17; Luke 5:27–32.
[212]   See Matthew 5:20; 15:12–14; 16:6–11; 21:45; Mark 8:15; 12:38–40; Luke 11:39–44; 12:1; 16:14 20:46–47.
[213]   See Matthew 22:15–22; Mark 12:13–17; Luke 20:20–26.
[214]   See Matthew 9:2–8; 12:9–13; 21:14–17; Mark 2:1–12; 3:1–6; Luke 5:17–26; 6:6–11; 13:10–17;, 14:1–6; John 5:1–18.
[215]   See Matthew 9:14–17; 15:1–20; Mark 2:18–22; 7:1–13; Luke 5:33–39.
[216]   See Matthew 22:41-45; Mark 12:35-37; Luke 20:41-44.
[217]   See Matthew 12:3-7; 9:32-34; 12:22-32; 21:23-27; Mark 11:27-33; Luke 20:1-8.
[218]   See Matthew 23:1–36; Mark 12:38–40; Luke 20:45–47.

was buried in the tomb of Joseph of Arimathea (*a respected member of the council*) with Joseph and Nicodemus preparing the body for burial.[219]

Although Jesus worshipped in the Temple and taught in the synagogues, he was very clear that the political powers represented by Rome, the Sanhedrin, and the religious establishment had no sway over him. Instead, he proclaimed the Kingdom of God that was separate and apart from an allegiance to Caesar[220] or to any other human institution. He spoke often of the Kingdom that is here, now, whenever and wherever he is present;[221] and of the same Kingdom that is always coming. It is the hope of the world. And yet it is not of this world. In fact, it isn't a place or a country at all but is the character and intention of God revealed in Jesus Christ.

How is the Kingdom of God relevant in the twenty-first century?

Although we are different from ancient Israel in many ways, we do seem to share their hope (*and delusion*) that the right leaders will solve all our problems or, at least, give us someone to blame if things don't go well. And what happened so very long ago feels strangely modern as daily headlines tell us that we too seem to have lost the ethical code that requires decency, honesty, compassion, and mutual respect in our personal and business dealings, especially in our communications with one another about the hot-button issues of politics.

Just like ancient Israel, we *do* keep horses—our military, the stock market, the rule of law, governing bodies, foreign alliances, the

---

[219]   See Matthew 27:57; Mark 15:43; Luke 14:1; 23:51; John 3:6–8; 19:38–39.

[220]   In Mark 12:17 Jesus says, "Give to the emperor the things that are the emperor's, and give to God the things that are God's." (See also Matthew 22:20 and Luke 20:25.)

[221]   See Matthew 10:7; Luke 10:8-11; 17:20-21; John 18:36; Romans 14:47; 1 Corinthians 4:20.

global economy—all the systems we have created to give us protection, comfort, prosperity, and power. As our horses stumble and disappoint, people all across the political spectrum say the same thing: "Let our leaders go out before us and fight our battles. And please, God, let it be someone who agrees with me!"

Let's face it. The Kingdom Jesus talked about expects an impossible righteousness that is especially difficult for Americans who are fiercely independent and uncomfortable with the idea of submitting to any sovereign or even to an elected official with whom we disagree. And yet how do we pray, "Thy Kingdom come . . ." and mean it in any way that matters?

First, we recognize this is not just a metaphor where our best hopes and wishes are hoped and wished for while the vast secular space around us is where "real" living takes place. The Kingdom of God is a fact made present in Jesus Christ. This Kingdom is not the United States or any other nation or any partnership, league, or coalition of nations. It is the all-inclusive commonwealth of God's redeemed (*and redeeming*) communities whenever and wherever Jesus Christ is present. And we are citizens by the same invitation and grace extended to all who willingly accept God's sovereignty and who follow Jesus Christ with bold compassion and humble service.

Second, we accept that the Kingdom of God is made up of men, women, and children; neighbors and strangers; colleagues and competitors; the likeable and the wearisome; right, left, and everything in between—all remarkable because they are Christ's own. And together we feed the hungry, clothe the naked, give clean water to the thirsty, show mercy to the outcast, offer forgiveness and love to one another, even to those we would rather not love or forgive. Why? Because he did it and told us to "go and do likewise." In short, the Kingdom of God is people who continue to do the work that Jesus started. The Kingdom of God is us—all of us.

Third, we understand that any earthly order we create, *at its best*, is a pale imitation of God's order. But this is where we find ourselves: called by God (*in spite of our inadequacies*), invited by Christ (*whose love transforms us*), and led by the Spirit (*who inspires and empowers us*).

Finally, as we participate in the political process, we acknowledge that if we claim to be Christians we have *two* citizenships:

As Americans, we exercise our rights (*all of them!*), and we should. We fulfill our responsibilities to obey laws and to engage in reasoned and respectful debate so the political process may push (*or pull*) our cities, counties, states, and nation toward better choices. We participate so the justice, peace, and compassion that Jesus taught (*and lived*) remain part of the agenda.

As citizens of God's Kingdom, we remember that God is never contained in our small spaces but hovers over, around, and through us, telling us that no king, no elected leader, no person can go out in front and do for us what we—with Christ—can and should do together. We accept that the justice, peace, and compassion that Jesus taught (*and lived*) are not things we can buy or sell or legislate or win through conflict or vote into being. They can only be lived by each of us every day.

Jesus kept the Kingdom separate and apart from politics for a reason.

The clear distinction Jesus made between God's Kingdom and the earthly seats of political and religious power reminds us that we always are in danger of creating institutions in the name of God that, in reality, serve our own ends. This applies to us in the twenty-first century as much as it did in biblical times. That's why we would do well to sift carefully through political rhetoric in order to separate what is biblically and Spiritually true from what we would like to believe based on our individual and collective traditions, preferences, and agendas.

In their wisdom, the Founding Fathers recognized the need to put some constitutional space between religion and political power, just as they rejected the idea of a religious test for citizenship and public office. Many of them had experienced firsthand the tyranny of a state church over the conscience of faithful people. They also knew what history says can happen when religion and politics become too closely aligned: Religion almost never elevates politics but is more likely to become corrupted by it and produce the likes of the Spanish Inquisition. Or the alternating torture and executions of Protestants and Catholics as monarchs came and went in Tudor England. Or the Salem witch trials. Or Adolf Hitler's killing spree that took place without opposition from the German Christian church and cost the lives of Dietrich Bonheoffer and millions of other human beings. Or any other forms of religious prejudice, persecution, or persuasion that happen in ways that are obvious or subtle.

In my lifetime, the candidacy of John F. Kennedy raised angry (*and ugly*) reactions from people who felt that no Roman Catholic *could* hold high office in America because they were not Christian and because all our freedoms would be lost to the Pope in Rome. All these years later, we know that Roman Catholics *are* Christians, and we still wrestle as a people (*without outside help*) to decide the complicated issues that determine where personal freedoms end and collective freedoms begin. Participating in the process are people who profess to be Roman Catholics, Greek Orthodox, mainline Protestants, no denomination, Jews, Latter-Day Saints, Muslims, other religions, and no religion at all, serving in elected offices all across the country.

In my lifetime, the question about having prayer in public schools propelled the country into a heated, emotional outrage—at least it did in my town and around the kitchen table at my house. I was in the sixth grade, and we started each day with the Pledge of Allegiance, a prayer, and a Bible study led by the teacher (*who also happened to be my Sunday school teacher*). When the prayer and Bible study were removed from the schedule, my father declared "the end of democracy as we know it." And I guess he was right. "Democracy as we know it" either had been irredeemably diminished, *or* it had expanded to respect those who had been left out before. It all depended on where you were standing.

Without trying to be disrespectful, I said, "Dad. You're OK with the prayer and Bible study in my class at school because the teacher also is my Sunday school teacher. Tell me, how would you feel if she were Catholic?"

"Well, she isn't!" he sputtered.

"Then how would you feel if she were Jewish?"

He didn't have an answer.

Like it or not, we both came to understand, or at least accept, that freedom *of* religion (*the right to worship in ways that feel faithful to us*) also implies freedom *from* religion (*not being required to observe or participate in worship that does not feel faithful to us*).

From a practical point of view, power and intimidation simply are not effective tools to achieve conversion—or submission—to worship and beliefs that people just don't feel. Ask any parent of a teenager who is rebelling against religion. You may get the body into church, but not the soul. The same principle applies to the use of judicial and legislative power in any way that requires the public as a whole to live according to the beliefs of a particular congregation or denomination or branch of the world's faiths. The usual comeback to this logic is that exposing someone to "the truth" may not produce immediate results, but it can have an impact later. Yes, it does. As a pastor, I have come across many people who are still wounded by their youthful experiences with organized religion that operated just this way. As a result, they resist the idea of going through any church doors, except for weddings, funerals, and the occasional high holy day when they happen to be visiting with parents who are still faithful church members.

For Jesus, the issue of who has authority in matters of religion was not about freedom *or* power. It was about God.

The prayer he taught his disciples (*and us*) says, *"Your kingdom come. Your will be done, on earth as it is in heaven."*[222] With this statement, he (*and we, whenever we pray this prayer*) makes bold claims: The Kingdom belongs to God—not to us. Those who are part of the Kingdom put God's will above their own. And the Kingdom is here on earth, where God's will is accomplished (*as surely as it is in heaven*). In short, the Kingdom and those who are part of it live within the sovereignty of God over whom there is no greater power. For that reason, it should not be confused or comingled with human political power—no nation, no region, no state, no commonwealth, no city, no town.

The impulse to use judicial and legislative means (*even with the best of intentions*) to impose particular expressions of faith in the public arena is not just an infringement on someone's freedom of religion. It is a way of saying that the Gospel message isn't compelling enough on its own to change lives, that we are ineffective messengers without some political force behind us, that God isn't powerful enough to work out Divine purposes on earth without the help of institutions we have created. In short, it is an affront to the sovereignty of God.

Relitigating the infinite possibilities of *"who has the right to make who do (or not do) what"* does little to show anyone the character and purpose of God revealed in Jesus Christ. There must be a better way.

A friend shared this story she heard Bishop Desmond Tutu tell about something that happened when he was a young boy in South Africa:

One day, as he and his mother were walking along a dusty road, they saw coming toward them an Anglican priest. As they passed each

---

[222]   Matthew 6:10.

other, going in opposite directions, the man tipped his hat to Desmond Tutu's mother. He didn't have to. Most people wouldn't have. After all, these people were invisible. But he tipped his hat. That simple act had a profound impact on the young boy—that someone would acknowledge their existence, their humanity, and their worth. Desmond Tutu said, in that moment he saw the Kingdom of God and knew it was a place where he might be a citizen, with rights and privileges and responsibilities. Such a simple act! And yet in that moment, an insignificant black boy and a white Anglican priest transcended the cruel political oppression of apartheid, and the whole world was changed.

God doesn't need to co-opt political power in order to change the world. Faithful Christians following the example of Jesus Christ have the power to do it every day. And God's people can change politics. Not by aligning religion with political power in order to carry out one group's idea of the great commission. Christians can change politics by engaging Biblical principles to change political discourse:

- When politicians and media personalities play on fear to immobilize and influence voters and viewers, Christians can remind us that God does not mean for us to live in fear, and that faith is the antidote for fear.

- When campaign rallies and speeches from the halls of Congress use anger and hyperbole to activate (*and enrage*) people, Christians can speak with reason and facts, remembering that Jesus said anger and slander are sins on the order of murder, because they tear apart the fabric of community.

- When debates heat up around all those issues that ultimately come down to wealth and poverty, Christians can follow the example of Jesus Christ and become compassionate advocates for people up and down the economic ladder. In their personal lives, Christians can make choices that lean toward the

Abundant Wealth that comes from God and brings with it a peace the world cannot offer.

• When crowds attack and demonize the Other, Christians can remind us that Jesus reached out to people who were excluded from belonging anywhere because they were "different"— separate from the mainstream and "not our kind of people." He made them his kind of people and said, "If you're with me, you have to understand that these folks are coming too." At the very least, Christians can think and talk about people who are *not* us in ways that honor the sacrifice Jesus made *for* us—all of us.

• When there is an impulse to engage political power to help with the challenging work of taking the Gospel into the world, Christians can remind us that no king, no president, no person can go out in front and do for us what we—with Christ—can and should do together. Christians can help us understand that the justice, peace, and compassion Jesus taught (*and lived*) are not things we can buy or sell or legislate or win through conflict or vote into being. They can only be lived by each of us every day.

Tell me, Christian, what act of kindness and decency might you and I do this day or this week so someone may see the Kingdom of God in us and feel it is a place where he or she can become a citizen, not invisible, but valued and worthy?

Tell me, Christian, into which unlikely stranger's face will you and I search for a spark of the Divine that may show us the Kingdom of God? For whatever we do to live, justice, peace, and compassion is never a small thing and is even now at work in the world, building God's Kingdom.

Summary: From the beginning, the Creator God worked through leaders, prophets, judges, and kings to shape the men and women created in God's image into a people who could be worthy of that image. To address human tendencies toward selfishness and division, God gave the Torah—the Law—to provide structure and guidance for living together in community.

However, people seldom have been able to apply God's instructions *for* their lives *to* their lives. All too often, the religious institutions that should lead people in worship and faithful living become too closely aligned with political institutions that should provide order and fairness among people in their civic life together, resulting in the corruption of one or both.

Jesus Christ introduced a third option: the Kingdom of God that is here, now, whenever and wherever he is present. It is the hope of the world. And yet it is not of this world. In fact, it isn't a place or a country at all but is the character and intention of God revealed in Jesus Christ. Those who are part of it live within the sovereignty of God over whom there is no greater power. And it should not be confused or comingled with any state or nation.

The Kingdom Jesus talked about expects an impossible righteousness that is especially difficult for Americans who are fiercely independent and uncomfortable with the idea of submitting to any sovereign. And yet how do we pray, "Thy Kingdom come . . ." and mean it in any way that matters?

We begin by recognizing that it is not just a metaphor but is the all-inclusive commonwealth of God's redeemed (*and redeeming*) communities whenever and wherever Jesus Christ is present. We accept that the Kingdom of God is people—including us—who continue the work Jesus started. As Christians, we acknowledge that we have two citizenships:

As Americans, we fulfill our responsibilities to obey laws and to engage in reasoned and respectful debate so the political process may push (or pull) our governing bodies toward better choices.

As citizens of God's Kingdom, we accept that the justice, peace, and compassion Jesus taught (*and lived*) are not things we can buy or sell or legislate or win through conflict or vote into being. They can only be lived by each of us every day. And part of that living can change politics by changing political discourse for the better.

Jesus has the last word:

> *"Bring me a denarius and let me see it." And they brought one.*
>
> *Then he said to them, "Whose head is this, and whose title?"*
>
> *They answered, "The emperor's."*
>
> *Jesus said to them, "Give to the emperor the things that are the emperor's, and to God the things that are God's."*
>
> *And they were utterly amazed at him.* (Mark 12:15–17)

Acknowledgments

This book has been shaped by parents who guided and encouraged me; teachers who answered my questions and gave me questions without answers; bosses who let me try wings that none of us knew for certain would work; the seminary faculty who had more information and wisdom than I could learn; pastors who inspired me and colleagues in ministry who keep me in awe of this work we do; congregations who have allowed me to serve them; my son Mike, who taught me about love and forgiveness; dear Aunt Jane, who gave me her hospitality and kitchen table where most of this came to life; and Raymond Summerlin, who showed me that living is a daily act of courage, and dying is a holy moment (I still wear his robe).

I am deeply grateful for kind and generous friends who listened while I wrestled with ideas and read as I wrote: Bob Blair, Judy Carlson, Kelly Crow, Pat Goldberg, Glenda Hollingshead, Mim Oman, Dodie Rossell, Patricia Valentine, and David Ross, who challenged me to make it better. Special thanks to R.M. Sexton.

Mostly, I thank the man in his plaid flannel shirt and honest work clothes whose goodness and decency still surround me. Without saying a word, he passed on his wisdom that woods and streams and animals and birds are heartbeats of God. Nothing we want to hide or change can justify being dishonest. No life is small unless we live it that way. Everyone deserves respect. Being dead certain is a good sign you need to look harder. Learning is like breathing; when it stops, you die. Life gives us unlimited opportunities to do some kindness for someone. And love really can be unconditional. He was Lewis Miller Smithson, my grandfather.

Notes

Much of the content of this book grew out of sermons and seminars delivered over the years. Therefore, it has been informed by books and articles, classes and seminars, and lively discussions with friends and colleagues – especially Raymond Summerlin who gave me every Saturday morning while he lived to explore the great mystery of what it means to be God's people.

In an effort to let the Bible speak for itself, I chose not to engage in specific research while writing; but am grateful for the following books *(among many others)* in my study that have helped shape my thoughts over time:

George Arthur Buttrick, editor, *The Interpreter's Dictionary of the Bible,* (four volumes), (New York, New York: Abingdon Press, 1962)

Shirley Guthrie, *Christian Doctrine,* (Louisville, KY: Westminster John Knox Press, 1994)

Leon R. Kass, *The Beginning of Wisdom: Reading Genesis,* (Chicago: The University of Chicago Press, 2003)

James Luther Mays, editor, *Harper Collins Bible Commentary,* (San Francisco: HarperSanFrancisco, 1988)

John A. Sanford, *The Kingdom Within:* The Inner Meaning of Jesus' Sayings, (New York, New York: Harper One, 1987)

Printed in the United States
By Bookmasters